The Informed Company

The Informed Company

How to Build Modern Agile Data Stacks that Drive Winning Insights

Dave Fowler
Matt David

Library of Congress Cataloging-in-Publication Data

Names: Fowler, Dave (Computer scientist), author. | Matt David, author.
Title: The informed company : how to build modern agile data stacks that drive winning insights / Dave Fowler, Matt David.
Description: Hoboken, New Jersey : Wiley, [2022] | Includes index.
Identifiers: LCCN 2021028324 (print) | LCCN 2021028325 (ebook) | ISBN 9781119748007 (paperback) | ISBN 9781119748021 (adobe pdf) | ISBN 9781119748014 (epub)
Subjects: LCSH: Data structures (Computer science) | Big data. | Cloud computing.
Classification: LCC QA76.9.D35 F69 2022 (print) | LCC QA76.9.D35 (ebook) | DDC 005.7/3—dc23
LC record available at https://lccn.loc.gov/2021028324
LC ebook record available at https://lccn.loc.gov/2021028325

Cover image: © Neo Geometric/Shutterstock
Cover design: Wiley
SKY10028766_091421

Contents

About This Book

Why Write This Book

Most comprehensive books on analytics architecture that we've found are over a decade old, most of them pre-cloud. Because there really isn't a modern equivalent to Kimball's seminal *The Data Warehouse Toolkit*, today's data teams have to reinvent the principles of building a data stack. Too often, they do this without guidance. To solve this problem, we have created a best-practices guide for bootstrapping and nurturing a technologically current data warehouse.

Who This Book Is For

We wrote this book for whoever values data and believes that informed companies are competitive. It's a book for the working professional who is creating a practical, modern data stack. It's for the lone analyst or the professional embedded in a team. It's for anyone interested in what design practices underlie robust data architecture, the kind that equips entire companies with business intelligence insights. At its heart, this book is written with collaboration in mind (Figure A.1).

Figure A.1 Data management is a collaborative process.

Who This Book Is *Not* For

This book is not written for "big data" professionals. To be clear, even large corporations like Doordash, Discord, and the owners of *The Financial Times* and *The New York Times* (all previous customers of ours) do not qualify as big data companies. As a rule of thumb, the big data label applies to data architectures with raw input that exceeds 100 GB per day.

No doubt, many elements of this text map onto the big data workflow, especially since warehouses support all sorts of tables, not just, say, event streams. However, our aim is to focus on the central pillars of a modern data stack, so that the widest set of readers can readily benefit from the information herein. In this spirit, we forgo recommendations for mega-scale architectures.

This book is not for AI-enabled teams and does not cover AI workflows, machine learning models, or real-time operational use cases. Instead, its goal is to provide best practices for building and maintaining a robust data analytics stack (i.e. the analytics foundation on which an AI workflow can be built).

If you are a small business that can run everything with Quickbooks and Excel, that ability is great. Data is important for all companies, but if these tools are already serving you well, the book may not offer helpful guidance. If you start exceeding the data capacity of Excel or bring in a data source that needs to be in a database to be analyzed, then keep reading.

Who Wrote the Book

This book was written by Dave Fowler and Matt David.

Dave Fowler has worked in BI for over a decade, and has always looked for ways to `JOIN teams ON data`. He wants to enable any working professional (not just data analysts) to explore and understand their data. As the founder and CEO of Chartio, Dave has spent the last 11 years leading the development of a self-service BI product that aims to do just that. Chartio's suite of tools make it easy for anyone at a data-driven business to browse their schemas, merge various data sources, and produce beautiful dashboards. In March 2021, Atlassian acquired Chartio and is integrating it into their platform.

Matt David has worked in product management and education for eight years. As data becomes a necessary skill for more and more jobs, he passionately advocates for data literacy among the workforce. As the current head of The Data School, he oversees the production of free, online resources focused on leveraging data within companies. Recent book topics include SQL optimization, data governance, and common analysis biases. Dave started The Data School, and together he and Matt have grown it into an important free resource for the data community. He previously worked at Udacity and General Assembly teaching analytics.

Dave and Matt decided to co-write this book after seeing how many people struggle when constructing data stacks and then trying to use them. This book was created with the support of many employees at Chartio. They graciously provided insights into how customers model their data and collected frequently asked data-infrastructure questions. Their contributions guided the production of this text.

Who Edited the Book

This book was reviewed and edited by Emilie Schario, Mila Page, and David Yerrington. Emilie is the head of data at Netlify and previously helped build Gitlab's entire data organization. She regularly writes and speaks on all things related to modern data. Mila is a developer relations advocate at dbt Labs, the makers of dbt (data build tool). She helps data professionals learn and apply modern analytics-engineering practices, and is an organizer for Coalesce, the dbt Community's annual conference. David is a Data Science Consultant and was the Global Lead Data Science Instructor at General Assembly. He helps people around the world better leverage their data. Emilie, Mila, and David have shaped the narrative and content of this book. Their (sometimes) line-by-line feedback has ensured that we can proudly stand behind our recommendations.

Influences

We've drawn on several sources of information and opinion when writing this text. While at Chartio, we worked with hundreds of modern cloud-based customers. We've collected, implemented, and refined these practices ourselves, and through writing this book, vetted them further with partners and customers. We've also learned from the data community through dataschool.com, blogs like Tristan Handy's, and data-focused slack communities.

And lastly, it's worth noting and thanking some classic books that informed the previous generation of warehousing toolkits. We honor them by echoing their terminology and best practices wherever possible:

- *Agile Data Warehouse Design* by Lawrence Corr
- *The Data Warehouse Toolkit* by Ralph Kimball
- *Information Dashboard Design* by Stephen Few (my review here)

How This Book Was Written

This book originates in part from a project within The Data School (Figure A.2), a collection of free online books and interactive tutorials on managing and leveraging data (see dataschool.com). These resources are always expanding, much like the articles of Wikipedia: each round of updates sees our ebooks cover additional topics, go deeper on established ideas, share more real-world examples, and better deliver that content. Our goal is to maintain and improve these resources and keep them modern.

Figure A.2
Source: The Data School

Few are complete "experts" in all of the areas of modern data governance, and the landscape is changing all of the time. If you have a story to share, or a chapter you think is missing, or a new idea, email us. Even if you don't know what specifically to share, but you don't mind sharing your story, please reach out as we are particularly interested in adding real-world experiences and insights.

There is already too much jargon in the data world, often created by talented vendor marketing teams. We try to stick with the most common and straightforward words that are already in use. For any jargon we do find necessary, we include a definition.

There are many books for the old ways of working with data. We're highlighting current best practices here, so we ignore outdated terminology and techniques. In a few cases where it is beneficial to talk about industry evolution—like the change from ETL to ELT—we teach ELT and discuss the choice in a separate chapter.

Almost every part of this book could be contentious to someone, in some use case or to some vendor. In writing this book, it is tempting to bring up the caveats everywhere and write what would ultimately be a very defensive and overly explained book. We believe this type of book is way less useful for people seeking straightforward advice. Where we have a strong opinion, we don't argue it; we just go with it. Where we think the user has a legitimate choice to make, we pose those options.

This book aims to provide a broad overview and general guidelines on how to set up a data stack. We intentionally gloss over the details of launching a Redshift instance, writing SQL, or using various BI products. That would clutter the text, repeat what's already on the internet, and make the read quite stale.

How to Read This Book

The book starts with a quick overview and decision charts about what the stages are and what stage is appropriate for you.

This book is structured with a section for each of the four stages, and if you'd like, you can jump ahead to the stage you're at.

Not every company needs the entirety of this book. As a growing company's data needs expand, more and more of the book becomes valuable. Note, though, many best practices presented at each stage appear when they start to be relevant. These practices assume they are useful from the point they appear in the book, onward, to avoid redundancy. So it may benefit you to at least skim those earlier stages even if you and your company are further ahead.

At the end of the book we have a section where we describe what has changed in the data world that makes this new architecture relevant and performant. We avoid explaining how our recommendations differ from previous practices like Kimball Dimensional modeling so as not to clutter the experience. Such discussions are necessary, however, and we've put them in this last section of the book.

Lastly, throughout the book you will see the following icons:

 Definitions

They are related to a term found on the same page. For example, on this page, the term "data lake" is mentioned. A data lake is a staging area for several data sources.

 Protips

Protips expand on an idea or provide additional information about a topic related to what you read within a given chapter.

Foreword

In 2015, I used a product called Amazon Redshift. At the time, I had spent the prior 15 years of my career in a variety of roles all centered around their use of data, from analytics to marketing to operations. And while I considered my data competency my biggest professional differentiator, I had also become deeply frustrated. For all of the supposed progress in the data ecosystem, it was still slow, hard, and expensive to get insights out of data.

But my first experience with Redshift is where that all changed for me. I have such a visceral memory of the first hour I spent with the product: queries I ran returned so fast that *it seemed like absolute magic*. I had spent years and years of my career writing queries and waiting for the MacOS "spinner" icon to stop spinning. Now, all the sudden, these same queries weren't 20% faster. . .they were 10 to 100 to 1000x faster. I felt like I had superpowers.

I'll let Dave and Matt actually explain *how* the modern data warehouse can achieve these types of performance results, but for now, just trust me that it can and does. Given that, the fascinating question is actually: *what does this mean for people like you and me?*

What kind of "people" do I mean? You know—people who are involved in making decisions at companies and want to use data to help us. People who likely over the years have acquired a variety of data skills, whether that's Excel VLOOKUPs, Google Analytics dashboards, SQL, or any of a thousand other options. People who have always felt like *it shouldn't be so hard to do basic stuff* when it comes to data (but of course, for some reason, it always has been).

What I've come to realize in the years since my initial experience with Redshift is that the modern data stack has exactly two very important impacts for us:

1. With this far better tooling, we can grow our impact on the organizations we work for *dramatically*. I'm going to say something really stupid and obvious, but: **if your queries return 100x faster, you can know 100x more stuff.** And that means that you'll just be tremendously more valuable in the insights you're able to provide and the decisions you can make.

2. As a result of #1, our career options are just far, far greater. When I started my career, "data analyst" was a junior position that you attempted to graduate out of as quickly as possible to move onto other things. Now data analysts are high-leverage, strategic employees with earning potential that mirrors that of software engineers.

There really has been a change in what a single analyst is able to accomplish with some fairly simple tooling and some very accessible knowledge and skills. That single individual can now construct an entire sophisticated data infrastructure by plugging together some inexpensive off-the-shelf tools, and then get to work getting insights. Or, that individual can operate as an integral part of a large and sophisticated data team, forming a part of the nervous system for the modern enterprise. The same technology, same skill sets, same knowledge is required regardless how big or small the organization.

This is the modern data stack. To harness its power, you need to know SQL (learnable a day!) and you need to know some basic best practices that folks like the authors of this book have been deep in the weeds developing and recording over the past half-decade.

It's surprisingly achievable—one of the magical things about these tools is just how little advanced technical knowledge is required.

This book provides the foundational knowledge you'll need to navigate the modern data stack. From there, you'll be able to dive in yourself, get your hands dirty, and start asking questions of your fellow practitioners. And when you do, make sure to head over to join me in the dbt Community—my Slack handle there is @tristan and I'd love to hear from you!

Introduction

Knowledge is power. Knowing more about your surroundings, like which fruit is safe to eat and which will harm you, keeps us safe and successful. Knowing more about the relationships between events, like the inverse relationship between washing hands and influenza outbreaks, minimizes inevitable difficulties. And knowing which strategies lead to success, like which mass-reforestation strategies lead to sustainable ecosystems, helps us optimize our efforts. In the modern world information on our environment is often in the form of data.

Whether by an individual or a team, data used intentionally and critically is a key part of success. While it's true that anyone can get lucky and stumble upon the right answer, having an idea of which tactics confer the most stability or which metrics indicate big opportunities for growth can drive teams forward quicker.

Our thesis is this: being informed implies being successful. But what does it mean for a person or an organization to be informed exactly? If you are sufficiently informed, you can make decisions with a sense of conviction that your thinking is correct a majority of the time. In the end, your gut feeling (intuition) factors into decision making. However, with well-organized and accessible information added into the mix, your "gut" can make more thoughtful (and better) decisions.

On the other hand, bad decisions are the result of not knowing enough: not knowing the root causes of numeric anomalies, not knowing where there is potential to invest more capital, and not knowing what the next few months could look like based on previous quarterly performance. Intuition is a powerful and necessary tool, but we believe that the individual and the company owe it to themselves to hone their intuitions. We believe that anyone with access to performance metrics should integrate that information into their decision making. Being informed is a key part of the puzzle to avoiding bad decisions. But what does it look like to be informed in the twenty-first century?

Companies and their operations continue to become more digitized. Companies no longer have direct access to each customer and must increasingly rely on data to improve and compete. So, organizations end up tracking a lot of data taken from many input streams. But why are so many teams struggling with organizing and leveraging insights from their data? We believe that the problem begins with tooling. We believe that the modern data workflow requires a data stack and operational structure that is ready for today's challenges.

In this book, we will outline what the modern data stack looks like starting from a brand-new startup all the way through a data-driven enterprise. We will cover architectures, tools, team organizations, common pitfalls, and best practices. Armed with these, we are confident that your team can identify the evolving needs of your business and implement solutions in your data infrastructure.

Merging Business Context with Data Information

There is a chasm between the people who know the technical aspects of how to work with data and the people who know the context behind that data. The technical people can write structured query language (SQL), whereas the business people know which marketing campaigns they've run and what types of users comprise

Figure I.1 Business
context vs technical
know how chart.

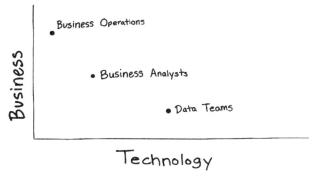

an analysis. This creates friction between the stakeholders who want access to data insights (without always knowing what that data looks like) and the analysts who know their data but not all of its history or significance.

A modern data stack seeks to bridge that gap. It enables an organization, not just analysts, to work with data. The modern data stack combines disparate input sources into a single understandable format and then stores that data in a single location that a business intelligence (BI) product can connect to. It should provide the information they need at their fingertips, and it should help everyone ask more questions. The modern data stack should empower teams to organize around a key performance indicator (KPI) and make decisions using data (Figure I.1).

Here are examples of being uninformed versus being informed:

Marketers who keep doubling down on all of their channels versus the ones who iterate or drops them depending on the success and failure of each campaign.

Sales leaders using anecdotes to support what type of customers they should target versus ones who know what customers are coming in and which are closing and can focus their teams accurately on the biggest opportunities.

Support persons who respond to an issue with "what browser are you using?" versus ones who have all of the error information, including the browser details, the account information, and recent actions.

Journalists writing about what matters to them versus ones who can see what resonates.

Product managers who justify their feature by showing the initial results versus ones who set up a test and let the data speak for itself.

Getting data into an understandable format that everyone has access to makes technical and business people *collaborators* rather than adversaries. It empowers everyone in the organization to make more informed decisions. This book aims to show how to set up a data stack to do just that.

The Four Stages of Agile Data Organization

After working with thousands of companies, we recognized four distinct stages of agile data organization (Figure I.2). Each of these stages has best practices and guidance on how to progress further "up the stack."

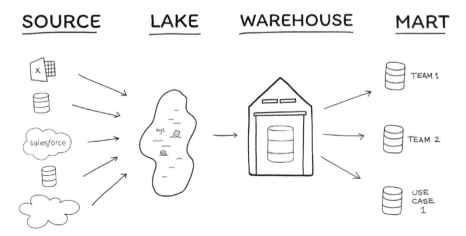

Figure I.2 The four stages of agile data organization represent a process that describes the lifecycle of data management.

This book maps onto these stages:

1. Source
2. Lake
3. Warehouse
4. Mart

Each vertical stage pictured could be what a company needs, depending on the resources, size, importance, and needs of data within an organization. Not every company needs all four stages. If a business gets the insights they need while in the source stage, then they should stay in the source stage. Likewise, a company may find it needs a lake to combine all of its data together but *may not* need the transformations implied in later stages of warehouse development.

Let's begin with an overview of each step.

Stage 1. Sources

Many teams only have a few data sources and commonly manipulate and visualize data in Excel or Google sheets. Two common sources that company products run on are Google Analytics and "transactional" database(s), such as PostgreSQL or MySQL. If only a few people at a company need to work with data sources, it's possible to set them up with direct or replica access; it's more agile and straightforward for them to work with the data directly.

We discuss how to configure proper access to data and how to lay the foundation for future organization into a single, unified collection of company data. We also discuss best practices when using tools like in-app dashboards, spreadsheets, SQL, and BI solutions. Behind these assertions is the principle that teams should be vigorously deliberate when organizing their sources and picking their toolkit. Keeping this in mind not only makes analysts effective at dealing with data early on, but also prepares them to reorganize their input streams into a *data lake* later on.

This stage is right if:

- Only a few people are going to be working with this dataset.
- Data needs are minimal at the moment.
- Only a few small data sources exist.
- The only people who need to make new visuals are fairly technical.

It's time for the next stage if:

- Data is accessed from multiple places/applications.
- There are needs for unique or combined charts/dashboards for cloud application sources like Salesforce.
- A growing number of people need access to data.
- There are performance issues.
- Data is getting too big for a transactional database to operate efficiently.
- Nontechnical users need to create charts without help.

Stage 2. Lake

Once companies must run analyses on multiple sources of data, each of which need joining, filtering, and manipulation, a company must move to a data lake. Blended data sources enable several actors in an organization to query a large subset of the company's complete data. In turn, funneling various sources into a data lake supports database performance at a reasonably large (not necessarily "big data") scale.

A central motivation for a data lake lies with the need for piping data to business intelligence tools. For example, when working with data from Salesforce, Hubspot, Jira, and Zendesk, each service has its own in-app dashboards and unique data application programming interfaces (APIs). Configuring input data streams for each business tool is a confusing, time-consuming, and unsustainable workflow. It cannot really be done, especially at scale. Likewise, performing in-house analyses across various sources can wildly complicate otherwise simple queries. On the other hand, having a data lake, which holds all relevant data in one place, allows analysts to use straightforward SQL queries to obtain business insights.

The central challenge faced by companies in the lake stage is knowing what toolset and methodology will unify and (safely) store your data. Companies looking to combine their data also run into performance issues, which we offer solutions to. And perhaps most important of all, choosing an architecture during lake development informs how easy (or hard) it will be for a company to build their future *data warehouse*.

This stage is right if:

- There's a need for unique or combined charts/dashboards for cloud application sources like Salesforce.
- A core set of people can learn the ins and outs of the structure of the messy data.
- You're intimidated by data modeling. (Don't be: that's why this book exists.)
- There's no time for even light data modeling.
- Large datasets need performant queries.

It's time for the next stage if:

- More than a few people are going to be working with this dataset.
- A clean source of truth would eliminate integrity issues.
- There's a need to separate the structure of the data from the always-changing transactional sources.
- There's a need to adopt DRY (Don't Repeat Yourself) principles.

Modeling

Data requires transformation so that it is more usable by different people or systems within a database. Modeling refers to this process of making these transformations to the data.

 DRY

An acronym that represents a software design ethos that avoids repetitive patterns through modularity of design.

Stage 3. Warehouse (Single Source of Truth)

As more people begin to work with the data lake, questions begin to multiply: What data is where? Why? What particular criteria should queries use when looking for data insights? What do these schemata mean? Unavoidable complexities make it harder to obtain data, especially by less-technical colleagues. Even among in-house experts, more schemata and entities (i.e. tables and views) in turn cause more communication headaches. In time, the data lake serves all data but makes it harder to obtain the *right* data. It gets harder to write queries and share the knowledge within an organization.

All of these problems can be addressed with a clean and simplified version of the data, something we refer to as "a single source of truth."

This stage—creating a data warehouse—has historically been quite a nightmare, and there are many books written on how best to model data for analytical processing. But these days, there are more straightforward paradigms that have been tried and tested: ones that not only streamline having to document the oddities found across an organization's schemata but also save time in having to repeat, edit, and maintain messy "boilerplate" query steps (e.g. "every time you query the order's table, make sure to adjust all orders from England to be in local time").

In the data warehouse section of the book, we review how to clean data lakes and investigate standard practices for managing data complexity. In addition, we offer ways to establish an architecture with data integrity in mind. We provide modeling tool suggestions and an example SQL style guide. Finally, we give our recommendations for team structure, such as a lead to oversee this process and warehouse maintenance.

Warehouse

This stage is right if:

- More than a few people are going to be working with data.
- A clean source of truth would eliminate integrity issues.
- There's a need to adopt consistent structure on top of the data lakes.
- There's a need to adopt DRY principles.

It's time for the next stage if:

- The democratization of data would help others explore and understand data without help.
- It's time to teach and enable business users to be more effective.
- Projects exist that require different formats than what currently exist in the data lake.
- Having truly informed employees is vital to your company's competitive success.

Stage 4. Marts

Good news, your data is clean and the BI product speaks directly with tables in the warehouse. Using a tool like Tableau or Looker, non-analysts within the organization can self-serve their questions. By that, we mean they are empowered to engage with the data directly rather than needing to have an analyst build or run queries for them. This is excellent news: more people who use the data become increasingly informed, and everyone across the company can use data to their advantage.

But given enough time, hundreds of tables accumulate in a warehouse. Users become overwhelmed when trying to find relevant data. It's also possible that, depending on the team, department, or use case, different people want to use the same data structured in different ways. So while the meanings of individual fields are unified, the abstractions used by different departments have diverged.

To sort through these challenges, we progress to the data mart stage. These are smaller, more specific sources of truth for a team or topic of investigation. For example, the sales team may only need 12 or so tables from the central warehouse, while the marketing team may need 20 tables—some of them the same, but some different.

Just as a warehouse lead manages data warehouses, data marts benefit from being facilitated by mart leads. The mart lead helps educate and communicate subject matter expertise within the domain of each respective mart while supporting everyday maintenance tasks. Not only will further simplification of data into local marts improve usability, but the integrity of data also becomes easier to maintain. After all, the responsibility of maintenance distributes to mart leads rather than to a single person. The organization that leverages data marts effectively is an example of intra-company data literacy in action.

Mart

This stage is right if:

- The democratization of data would help others explore and understand data without help.
- It's time to teach and enable business users to be more effective.
- Projects exist that require different formats than what currently exists in the data lake.
- Having truly informed employees is vital to your company's competitive success.

It's time for the next stage if:

- The data mart stage is the final stage. There can be any number of marts, and there can be multiple levels of marts if needed. After implementing this stage, data arrives in a complete, well-architected, and governed stack that continually evolves to support an informed and competitive company.

STAGE 1
SOURCE
aka Siloed Data

Source Stage Overview

Modern businesses, even modest sized ones, generate heaps of data that comes in several flavors—product information, customer information, app performance, marketing expenditures, and more. A new business can work with data from production databases, product APIs, and financials directly from their sources.

Over time, as sources accumulate more data, the number of data channels grows as well. It becomes even more challenging to manage data across separate sources.

This section is about helping you work with sources. We talk about what sources are and what we can do with them. From there, we survey the tools commonly used to connect and investigate sources; for each example, we offer quick but tested thoughts on how these tools can be used by your team. We complete our discussion on sources by encouraging best practices on how to work with data during the source stage. We advocate for source replicas and streamlined data intelligence tools.

This stage is ideal for new companies or teams with minimal data needs. It is inexpensive and relatively easy to tool, implement, and maintain. While it is exciting to build out a sophisticated data stack, it is not necessary before circumstances require it. Over-engineering is a costly mistake. However, the methods discussed in Chapters 1, 2, and 3 set the stage for your future data lake and data warehouse that arise as the scale and diversity of your source data proliferate.

Chapter One

Starting with Source Data

When starting from scratch, keep in mind the potential for the data to grow and the usability needs of users in the future. In the beginning, sources are their own islands separated from each other. Data streams remain in their own "silo." When a data team is small, a collection of sources is easy to maintain and monitor. For example, to support new data teams, many data sources have their own built-in dashboards and reporting capabilities (see Salesforce, Heap, and so on).

While single-source data isn't all that powerful, it's not at all useless. Some everyday use cases of solutions built from single-source data include:

- Database queries that generate customer acquisition metrics.
- A dashboard that displays monthly sales featuring a downloadable spreadsheet.
- A custom web application that allows searching of referral traffic.

Siloed reporting does not yield the powerful data insights that more sophisticated teams need, but this is often where teams must start. The analyst's role becomes that of an instructor to stakeholders—the analyst must understand sources and support business stakeholders who read and interact with this limited data. An analyst may pull together numbers from separate comma-separated value files (CSVs) and run manual analysis in Excel or with basic SQL queries.

As we explore data sources, remember that analysts can do *much more* for their teams than work with business intelligence tools, Excel, and simple queries. In time, they can build abstractions on top of the data that make data accessible to other colleagues and self-servable (more on this in Stages 2 and 3).

Common Options for Analyzing Source Data

Data ends up in many different places, but the methods to analyze them boil down to application dashboards, Excel spreadsheets, SQL IDEs, cloud dashboarding tools, or business intelligence (BI). We proceed to touch on several common tools used for interacting with sources, giving a short judgment on when and how to use them (Figure 1.1).

Figure 1.1 Various methods for data analysis for data sources.

Get to Know Data with Application Dashboards

Many modern software as a service (SaaS) applications come built with a set of fixed dashboards and visualizations to showcase the data they are capturing (Figure 1.2). These charts are highly tuned to specific use cases and can be quite informative—and maybe meet all data needs. Some, like Salesforce, even have a customizable chart and dashboard creator built in to support ad-hoc querying. Many have custom query languages, too. These can go a long way, especially when there is no need to see this data in combination with other data. An additional part of the value proposition underlying these tools is vendor support staff, who help answer questions or fulfill special data needs.

One word of caution: keep an eye out for how often single sources of data need combining with other sources. Perhaps you often fulfill queries like "tell me what lead type creates the most customer support tickets," that is, business asks that require analysis across multiple sources. If your team finds themselves playing the part of "glue" between single sources all too often, it may be time to move to the Data Lake stage.

Figure 1.2 Example built in dashboard showing common metrics from Zendesk.
Source: "Zendesk"

Ask Interesting Questions with Excel

Most applications can export some of their data into CSV formatted files (Figure 1.3). Anyone with Excel or Google sheets can then import that data and analyze it. While this is an effective way to expand the questions that one can ask of data from applications, it is relatively manual and requires frequent updates to keep data current.

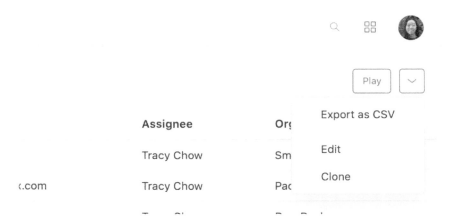

Figure 1.3 A basic export feature on a web services dashboard providing a CSV download.
Source: Microsoft

Query Databases with an SQL IDE

For data sources such as a production database, they can be queried directly from the command line, but this can get messy and hard to keep track of queries and results. We suggest setting up an integrated development environment (IDE) such as pgAdmin to better handle querying data within a schema (Figure 1.4). These tools have features that support writing queries (i.e. autocomplete), saving queries, and exporting data.

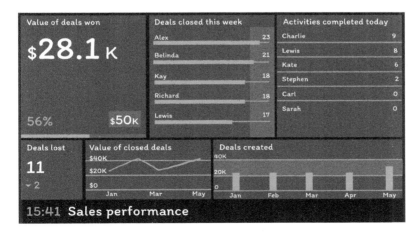

Figure 1.4 pgAdmin dashboard is a popular IDE for PostgreSQL.
Source: pgadmin.org

Visualize Data in the Office with Dashboards

Tools like Geckoboard or Grow receive data from cloud applications via APIs, then visualize that data in simple yet useful ways (Figure 1.5). These tools can provide data blended from multiple sources into a single dashboard.

These types of cloud dashboard tools often come with some helpful default dashboards and also look great on TVs around the office. They keep teams aware of what's going on. However, these solutions are very limited in their customizations.

Figure 1.5 Geckoboard like dashboard displaying standard sales metrics.

Toying Around with Analytics Products

Tools like Amplitude and Mixpanel (Figure 1.6) can help make product managers more self-sufficient by removing the need to involve engineering to add tracking events. Product analytics provides templated analysis and a GUI so no code is needed to ask questions of the data. This appears to be a great solution, but we would advise caution with these sorts of tools.

Unfortunately these tools are typically expensive and for every new event tracked you have to wait a few months to get the data you need. These events are typically already tracked in the application database but may be named and stored in hard to understand ways. In addition, product analytics tools are limited to data from the application, meaning we can't see revenue or other business metrics that exist in other sources. Product Analytics do not really scale to serve the data needs companies have.

Figure 1.6 Mixpanel cohort analysis.
Source: Mixpanel

Look at Data Through a Business Intelligence Tool

For the most power in working with source data, use a flexible self-service BI solution. For this stage, be sure to choose an agile product that supports direct SQL queries and ideally the ability to connect to and blend data from multiple sources.

The main benefits of adopting a BI solution with direct SQL capabilities include:

- Consistency of data access.
- Lower cost of operation.
- Portability of data to future systems such as data lakes.

When data sources aren't consolidated or cleaned and organized, these types of BI solutions are necessary but, on occasion, may require complex SQL queries. Tools like Looker and our very own Chartio support writing queries and managing custom dashboards (Figure 1.7).

Figure 1.7 Chartio Dashboard Executive Summary of Sales Metrics.
Source: CHARTIO

Chapter Two

The Need to Replicate Source Data

Each query, whether it's sent through a business intelligence tool, a SQL workbench, or something similar, requests data from a source. It takes technical resources, time, and computing energy to serve queries. This is especially relevant when running queries "against" a "production database" (see Figure 2.1), as too many queries, especially ones that take a long time to run, can bog down machinery (and don't forget how cluttered dashboards can cause many queries to run at once).

 Production Systems

A production system is any system that serves critical business functions to users. An example of a production database system is one that powers an application for users to buy this book

Figure 2.1 A production system should be used with care.

on the internet and handles credit card transactions. We advise against querying data directly from production systems due to its potential ability to interfere with your live application.

Newer businesses investigating their internal data tend to draw from live, or production, systems. In other words, they run analysis-type queries directly on their data sources. While this is okay for tools like Salesforce or Google Analytics, mainly because querying doesn't impact their performance at all, the same can't be said about on-premises or even cloud-hosted production systems.

Querying data on a production system carries the following risks:

- Slowing down the performance for all users and applications.
- Accidental data loss.
- Lowered system integrity.

We can mitigate these risks by creating a copy of the production system and only providing read-level access to those who are trying to analyze it (Figure 2.2).

Replicate Sources

We heartily suggest copying mission-critical data sources into copies with read-only access. All analysis queries should be run against those copies, or "replicas," as opposed to directly on production systems. For each replica created, access should be revoked from the original

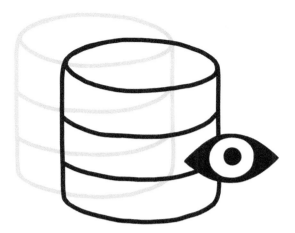

Figure 2.2 A cloned data source with read-only access.

source database. Grant access to the replica instead, so that relevant users within your organization can query the replica. Likewise, have visualizers talk to replica tables rather than product systems.

This read-only stand-in protects production databases so they are not violated by a mistaken INSERT or bogged down with frequent SELECT requests. It may seem excessive at first glance because of the indirection, but this step removes another point of failure in your business's application. We concede that although creating a read-only replica is straightforward for cloud providers with hosted databases like RDS, it can be challenging with other platforms. Moreover, we acknowledge that databases may double the costs of storing data, but they remove the risk of an analytic query affecting an application. It may be equally frustrating to experience a time delay between the transactions in your production database and transfer of those new records to the replica.

But again, no company wants to find itself with their central product, whether it's an e-commerce site or a patient scheduling system, crashing every time a dashboard is opened due to database conflicts (Figure 2.3). Moreover, the need for this has spurred cloud providers to improve the ease with which replicated tables can be created and automated.

Figure 2.3 It is dangerous to use a production system for non production purposes such as analytics.

Create Read-Only Access

Now that users have access to the replica, make sure they only have read-only access. This limits their interaction with the database to only be able to retrieve data, not to manipulate it. This will prevent a user from accidentally deleting, updating, or adding any data. The ability to manipulate the actual data on the database should be reserved for engineers.

Chapter Three

Source Data
Best Practices

After establishing an SQL-based BI tool to blend and analyze data, there are some best practices to keep in mind to support other people using the data. It's not crucial to spend too much time modeling or cleaning data at this point, but giving some direction can be invaluable at this stage.

Keep a Complexity Wiki Page

Data is inherently messy at the source stage and will be difficult for everyone to gain experience with and use. Since the amount of data sources is small, it is prudent to create a document or wiki page with warnings about known problems so others can navigate the data themselves.

Here are common data problems to document:

- Descriptions of poorly named columns and tables.
- Columns with nulls or mostly useless data.
- Business logic.
- Complex or confusing join paths.
- Old or unused columns and tables.

Snippet Dictionary

Another useful document to keep is a dictionary of base queries or SQL snippets for standard metrics (Figure 3.1). When working with unmodeled data, it's common to repeat a lot of the same filters and joins. It's helpful to conveniently copy paste/snippets when needed, rather than to recreate each time they're needed.

These can be stored on a wiki, an SQL file, or even as a dashboard of these queries saved as charts. With the right BI product, the dashboard method is ideal, because these snippets are available as starter charts that can be easily duplicated and adjusted.

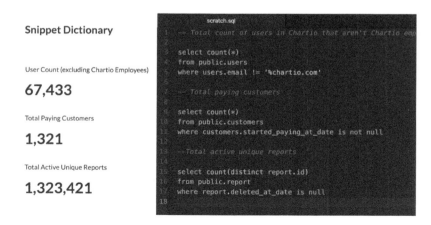

Figure 3.1 Using an SQL file in an editor to manage dashboard metrics.
Source: Chartio and Atom

Along with the snippets, it is a best practice to add comments describing the calculation of any metric. These snippets and comments are a good starting point for data models at the warehouse stage of agile data organization.

Use a BI Product

Modern BI products allow a user to conduct light modeling of the data at the BI layer. They contain schema editors that enable users to quickly rename fields, hide columns, specify join paths, and create custom columns or tables. While these small changes are easy to do if a lot of changes are necessary, consider moving all the way forward to the warehouse stage where modeling can be universally applied and leveraged.

In addition to SQL access, some BI products with drag-and-drop data explorers, such as Tableau Desktop or Chartio's Visual SQL (Figure 3.2), handle SQL writing automatically. This is especially useful for teams who are still getting their feet wet with writing raw SQL. Visual interfaces handle changing data format strings, join paths, new groupings, and unique dialects, all of this saving the new data team precious time spent googling and debugging.

At the data source stage, it's possible to be dealing with sources in multiple SQL dialects and a few different APIs. One of the most significant benefits of these visual interfaces is that they operate in the same way, regardless of the source, and that they write the correctly formed SQL.

These interfaces continue to be useful even after the data team has cleaned data into a lake and set up a warehouse, as others in the company can use these sorts of tools to explore data and self-serve data insights.

Figure 3.2 A custom SQL building feature, "Visual SQL" from Chartio.
Source: Chartio

Double Check Results

Whenever producing visualizations, unexpected or null values can make an analysis incorrect. Always do a quick review of the raw data by sorting each field to see if any data needs to be removed, ignored, or nulls/outliers updated so that the analysis is accurate.

 Finding Outliers with SQL

Using SQL, it's possible to quickly find outlier values by sorting a column in ascending or descending order. Use the Order by clause to investigate columns:

```
SELECT
  name, height
FROM
  table
ORDER BY
  height ASC
```

```
SELECT
  name, height
FROM
  table
ORDER BY
  height DESC
```

Keep Short Dashboards

People tend to keep adding more and more charts to existing dashboards. This leads to cluttered interfaces and less accessible information to non-subject matter experts (Figure 3.3).

Figure 3.3 A very long dashboard.

Usually, due to finding insights incrementally, the number of charts steadily increases, until the end result is a very long, disorganized dashboard running unique queries for each chart. Often, these queries rerun each time the dashboard is refreshed.

With a large dashboard, merely opening it to see one or two of key metrics can kick off hundreds of queries. Generally, it's best to organize a dashboard around a single question or goal and then break out multiple dashboards for follow-up questions and analyses (Figure 3.4).

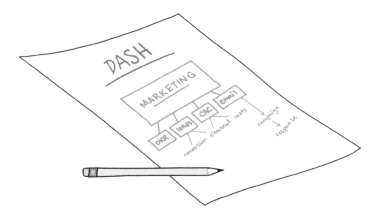

Figure 3.4 A simple dashboard outline.

 Blog Recommendation

We believe in keeping dashboards concise yet straightforward, so they deliver the maximum amount of information possible. A fantastic blog post on this practice and more we recommend is: *Best Practice: Keep Shorter Dashboards,* by Dave Fowler:

https://chartio.com/blog/best-practice-keep-shorter-dashboards/.

Design Before Building

Another common pitfall is starting a dashboard by exploring data first. Starting dashboard projects by only data exploration often leads to a collection of what seems like useful charts at first, but rarely are these charts worthwhile monitoring daily.

 Book Recommendation

An excellent online book that goes over how to avoid common pitfalls related to designing dashboards that we recommend is: *How to Design a Dashboard,* by Matt David (Figure 3.5):

https://dataschool.com/how-to-design-a-dashboard/.

Figure 3.5 The book cover for *How to Design a Dashboard*, by Matt David.

When creating key dashboards that need continuous monitoring, first spend some time with pen and paper outlining the most valuable charts and metrics. Brief sketches save time, allowing fast iterations, and result in a considerably more useful dashboard. Also, during the sketching process, define who uses the dashboard, which questions they want to answer, and which metrics would be useful. Lastly, deploy the dashboard and continuously iterate on this process with users who use the dashboard.

STAGE 2
DATA LAKE
aka Data Combined

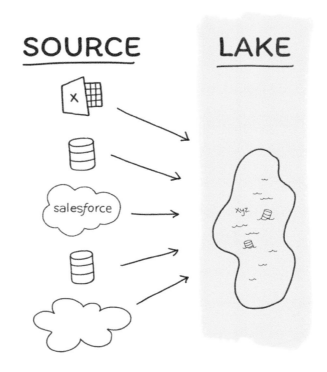

Lake Stage Overview

Your business keeps growing and, with it, the number of data sources that it draws from. The insights your team gets from these data sources continue to be useful, but it is increasingly harder to keep track of APIs, CSVs, and so on. Before too long, it will be more or less impossible to take on new data sources. It will become even more impractical to work with the sources you do have; there is too much manual reconciliation between disparate data sources. Something has got to change.

This section provides a roadmap and technical solution for escaping source hell. Here, we discuss the abstraction of a data lake. The actual idea itself is not too difficult to discuss, but there are a number of value propositions that come with this technique that may be immediately obvious. So, after taking time to investigate what data lakes and what source of engine would be suitable for my needs, we'll go down the list of what makes a data lake such a useful tool.

We discuss in detail what ELT is and why we believe it is a superior method for building data analytics ecosystems. We touch on a number of products out there and their pros and cons.

Lastly, we make time to explain the security and maintenance aspects of data lakes. It's our express goal to explain what a data lake is and what its employment entails.

Chapter Four

Why Build a Data Lake?

As we explored in the previous section, over time, teams see their sources of information proliferate. As business operations scale, so does the number of places data flows in from, or maybe the number of input channels remains unchanged but the size of those streams increases dramatically. This alone is challenging. Then remember that each source may run on a different system or be run by a different organization. Each source could have its own domain-specific dialect of SQL or API calls, its own default time zone, its own set of permissions and system for managing them, its own owners, and its own limitations on how the data within them can be queried or visualized. The siloed-off source model breaks down into a mess of disparate data.

A new abstraction layer is needed to make sense of this new reality. Consider that sooner or later, even if a team increases analyst headcount, it becomes impossible to sort and maintain sources. The key

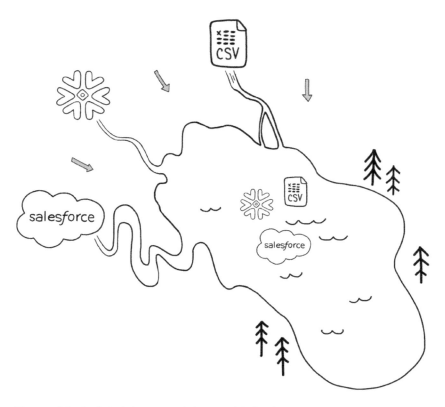

Figure 4.1 A data lake containing multiple data sources.

insight is that there should be one place where all data collects rather than sources all in different siloes. There should be a unified way (or ways) of requesting that data from this unified source.

Just like we recommended replicating production database systems, we encourage replicating all sources into a single data store. This collection of replicated source is called a *data lake* (Figure 4.1).

What Is a Data Lake?

The term *data lake* (the name taken from the lakes of pre-refinery crude oil which derricks dump extracted oil into) was created to contrast the term *data mart*, which describes orderly, siloed, and refined data (Figure 4.2). The bridge between marts, tailored for

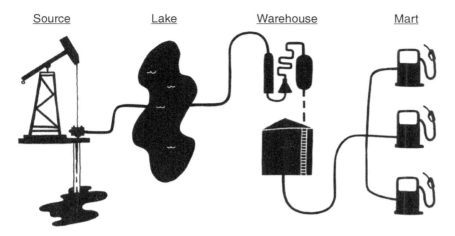

Source   Lake   Warehouse   Mart

Figure 4.2

special jobs, and the lake is called a warehouse. And because the warehouse will sit on top of your data lake, the shape of your data lake will inform the shape of your data warehouse. But in contrast to marts, data lakes are not refined or orderly. Instead, a lake's job is to solve the many distributed sources problem. We can bring further order later on when it's needed for intelligence insights.

Implementation-wise, a data lake is very often a database with its own set of rules and customers. In the current data landscape, lakes are nearly always hosted on a cloud database engine (Redshift, Snowflake, BigQuery, etc.). Unlike the transaction-first databases that support applications, the MySQLs of the world, cloud warehouses are designed with complex analytical queries in mind. Their job isn't to manage batch processing of INSERTS, UPDATES, and DELETES. Instead, they are designed to handle incredibly large amounts of data and optimize that data for analytics workloads.

Reasons to Build a Data Lake Summarized

One Technology

As data needs increase, it becomes harder and harder to work with data kept in silos, even when it seems to make sense that source data should be kept apart. For example, it may make sense from a product perspective that content marketing data should be in Hubspot, sales records should be in Salesforce, and trial engagement data should be in a transactional database. To analyze funnel and attribution models, however, these sources must be put together in some common data store. When all data resides in a single warehouse engine, queries can access all data in one language. Not only is the programming more straightforward, but also you make it easier to do cross-source analyses.

JOINing

In the source stage, we explained blending options with BI tools. A BI tool can connect to several sources and some can even combine these different sources together so that it is ready for visualization in a chart. But, the data processing capabilities of BI tools are limited. Many require data be prepared before being able to visualize it effectively.

After combining sources into a singular data lake, collective analysis over total organizational information becomes far simpler. Once data exists in the same place, queries can join across different sources, no additional loading required. The data lake kills the need to prepare sources for future joins. For example, a single ad-hoc query on a data lake can display how many tickets (from Zendesk) were filed by power users (from an application DB) who work at enterprise companies (from SalesForce). A lake makes joining data from disparate data sources much easier.

Robust Query Writing

The applications a business uses likely only offer transactional API access to the data. Usually, these applications are not optimized for reporting or analysis. So, unless the data is exported and put into some standard format, it becomes increasingly difficult to use that source in analyses. Sometimes, source-specific APIs can also become prohibitively expensive, if used directly for reporting. APIs often have a free tier in terms of how often and how much data you can request; then they limit usage unless you start paying them a fee.

On the other hand, a modern cloud warehouse engine comes equipped with several analytics-minded functions built into their native SQL dialect (Figure 4.3). These operations are efficient and cost effective. The cost of a query on your own database is typically much cheaper than API calls to SaaS applications. Querying from your own database will not only be faster but it will be cheaper.

Therefore, the cheaper and more sensible option to working with data from APIs is to *extract* it and then use an ELT product to *load* it into a data lake. Once loaded into the lake, you can query your data many times in many different ways using SQL (or another data processing language supported by the warehouse engine). Since you are not hitting the underlying source directly, you lose a touch of data freshness. But, this trade-off earns you speed and cost savings. It's possible to query with the power and flexibility of SQL or any BI product used—the costs don't increase considerably with each chart unlike multiple pings to the API the source was extracted from.

Figure 4.3 A dashboard using data from various data sources.

Performance

Source data might be from an actual production database, which could affect the performance of the application that it is powering. Queries that demand a lot of data and calculations such as aggregations are not optimally run on transactional databases (Figure 4.4).

Data lakes ideally handle these types of ad-hoc analytical queries independently of the production environment. It's possible to scale up resources on a data lake to be able to query data even faster. Remember that a data lake is a collection of replicas after all. That layer of indirection leads to a more fault-tolerant data stack.

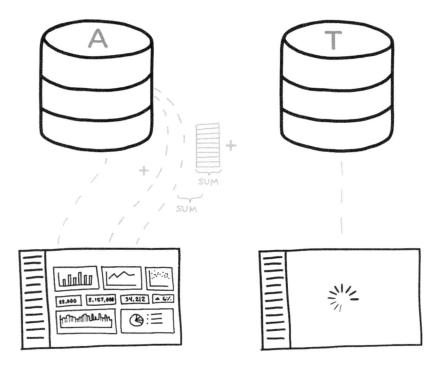

Figure 4.4 For dashboards that consist of large aggregations a transactional database is typically slower than an analytical database.

Future Development

Collecting all your sources into one data store is a necessary step for building the rest of the modern data stack. Doing this dramatically reduces the number of headaches suffered from analysis and reporting because many BI products intend to only draw from one source anyway. Some BI tools are able to blend sources in queries and charts, but it is still more performant (and scalable) to spend the time loading your sources into a data lake.

The value of this may not present itself so clearly, so let us explain with a quick peek into the next stage of developing an agile analytics stack. In the warehousing stage, much of your effort involves transforming tables and views in the data lake to be more clear and consistent. This enables more people to use it, causes fewer errors, and results in less duplication of work. This warehouse layer of transformations requires a data lake at its foundation.

Chapter Five

Choosing an Engine for the Data Lake

Lakes typically run on a different database engine than transactional source databases. As mentioned, transactional databases such as PostgreSQL or MySQL are optimized for doing the massive number of relatively simple queries that are required to support a working product.

Data lakes, however, are usually hosted on what is called a data warehouse engine, which is built for more complex analytical queries on larger volumes of data.

Think of transactional databases as a scooter, and data warehouse engines as a semi-truck (Figure 5.1). They're both valuable vehicles, but clearly have different jobs. It is impractical to deliver the mail door to door with a semi-truck, just as it is impractical to serve

Figure 5.1

thousands of small requests to different places per second from a data warehouse engine. The semi-truck is suited to deliver many tons of packages across the country to smaller distribution hubs, much like a data warehouse engine is suited to performing big analytical queries to a BI tool.

 What About Big Data?

Hadoop is a common big data framework for parallel computing with clusters. Hadoop is like a barge. It can haul a lot but not well and only down the river. Just avoid it. S3 is another big data option; it is like a train. It can be helpful for a bit but eventually you have to get it off the track and into highways. Only do this if you're hauling massive amounts of data. (If you have massive data, you know you have massive data.)

S3

S3 is the Simple Storage System provided by Amazon Web Services. It's designed to store files of all sizes providing access through an HTTP layer.

Standardizing a data lake on a warehouse engine solves a lot of immediate needs for performance and, at the same time, simplifies access through the unification of data sources. Not only are there plenty of warehouse engine service offerings, but the cost of these services has never been more affordable. Also, using a warehouse engine ensures technical simplicity for moving onto the warehouse project, as the cloud warehouse engine chosen will support future data transformations indicative of an increasingly mature data stack.

Modern Columnar Warehouse Engines

But why are data warehouses of today so much more powerful than the transactions engines that emerged earlier on? A central reason begins with the way transactional database engines store information on the hard disk of their host machine.

 Transactional Database

A row-oriented database optimized for the addition, update, and removal of records.

Transactional databases are optimized not only for performing reads and write operations safely but also for doing a whole lot of these operations *fast*. In particular, for an e-commerce site, the company web application may make hundreds of writes per second as new orders are placed by customers, items are added to virtual carts, and so on.

Note that writes and updates are operations performed on whole rows. For efficiency, these kinds of databases organize data by record, keeping all the bytes associated with a record in contiguous arrays in memory. However, when it comes to querying a row-oriented database, lots of irrelevant data may be accessed for aggregations and joins.

The nature of the technology itself frustrated the efforts of analysts to performance data analysis on large sets of data in a timely manner. Innovation in the underlying tech needed to occur before the modern analytics era could begin.

Fast forward to 2005 when a combined group from Brown University, Brandeis University, and MIT released a groundbreaking paper known as the C-Store paper, introducing a new column store architecture. That paper introduced new concepts that led to a new class of cloud-based databases, the kind that handle large sets of data and do it with extreme power.

 C-Store

A column-oriented database system developed by a team at Brown University, Brandeis University, Massachusetts Institute of Technology, and the University of Massachusetts Boston, including Michael Stonebraker, Stanley Zdonik, and Samuel Madden. Also referred to as a columnar or column-based database system. Storing data in columnar form on the disk track leads to more performance queries than on databases stored in rows.

This sort of warehouse engine works best for analytic workloads that require more substantial but less frequent queries than their transactional counterparts. Yet, analytics queries tend to be more complex than transaction queries and they are performed over more extensive datasets. Column-oriented (columnar) databases organize data by field, keeping all of the data associated with a

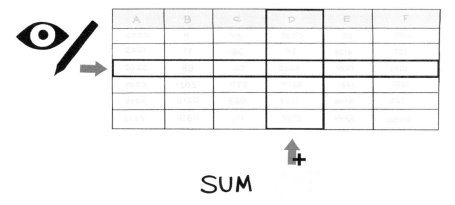

Figure 5.2 A transactional database can read and write rows quickly, and an analytical database can aggregate on columns quickly.

field next to each other in memory (Figure 5.2). Hence, the C-store model suits the analyst's workflow far better.

Columnar Storage Data Lakes

Columnar databases have grown in popularity and provide performance advantages for the analyst workflow especially. In practical terms, they are optimized for reading and *computing* on columns efficiently. Your lake should be built using a columnar database. After all, columnar storage has been optimized for analysis. The real question is what warehouse engine should your team use for your data lake?

Deciding Factors

When selecting the right data engine for an organization, the two main types of solutions are on-premises or cloud-based. More and more businesses are moving to cloud solutions to take advantage of the "as a service" model to save on hardware costs, which is where we'll focus in this section.

The most significant decision to make when moving from the source stage of agile data organization to the lake stage is which warehouse engine to use. Warehouse engine solutions come in different pricing structures, exist on and off accessible cloud infra-structures like AWS and GCP, scale differently, and have different maintenance requirements.

We find that it's best to make a decision based on:

- Pricing
- Ecosystem
- Performance/Scale
- Maintenance

There are a variety of database pricing models, from being based on storage to being based on the amount of data queried. Com-panies that are strictly using Amazon or Google as their software vendors may dictate the vendor choice as well.

The architecture of the data lake has implications on how it helps operations scale. Differences in the many types of lakes entail columnar versus row-oriented storage and having storage and compute together or separated. Maintenance requirements of a data lake may impact the decision as well.

Modern Warehouse Engine Products

Today, there are three dominant choices for cloud-based data ware-house engines: Amazon Redshift, Google BigQuery, and Snow-flake. Note: all of these are similar and based on the C-Store paper.

Amazon Redshift

Pros
Redshift (Figure 5.3) has the benefits of ease of use, speed, and cost. Being a part of AWS, there is full-service integration for the broad range of AWS services such as S3 for storage and Cloud-Watch for infrastructure monitoring. Redshift is generally cheaper

Figure 5.3

than Snowflake or BigQuery, with a couple of pricing options such as paying hourly per node or paying by the number of bytes scanned with Redshift Spectrum.

It's simple to set up and scale by adding nodes to a cluster, increasing storage to gain performance. It benefits from being similar in connection and SQL syntax to PostgreSQL.

Cons

Users can often run into concurrency issues with Redshift due to incomplete configuration or when there are high volumes of queries from many users accessing the database. Ongoing maintenance may be required with Redshift to resize clusters, define sort keys, and vacuum data.

Like many AWS services, there are ways to customize a configuration with workload management, compression, and partitioning. However, using these advanced features is not very out of the box. So although Redshift is powerful, it may require a dedicated resource from a data engineering team to optimize performance.

 Vacuuming

When deleting data from a database, it is not necessarily removed from storage right away. In some systems the data is "marked" as "dead" rather than completely removed. When processing new requests, additional work is required to filter "marked" data during future read operations. Over time, as more "marked" data accumulates, this ends up impacting read performance of requests. Vacuuming is a common maintenance task required by *some* warehouse engines that deletes "marked" data, generally improving performance.

Google BigQuery

Pros

BigQuery (Figure 5.4) is not bound by cluster capacity of storage or compute resources, so it scales and performs very well with increasing demands for concurrency (e.g. more users and queries accessing the database). As a fully managed database, BigQuery handles vacuums and resizing on its own, which can save time for data engineers and makes it easy to use and maintain. For businesses using Google products, BigQuery integrates well with Google Drive, Google Billing, and Google Analytics.

Cons

Cost is determined per query byte, making it difficult to budget or regulate for users who run ad-hoc queries against their data. To keep costs from getting out of control from ad-hoc queries, leverage BigQuery's cost controls. Implementing cost controls can restrict the amount of analysis that's performed because it limits the queries that potentially run. It also has some nonstandard syntax. While some prefer it, it does have a learning curve and a different way of working with it.

Figure 5.4

Figure 5.5

Snowflake

Pros

Like BigQuery, Snowflake (Figure 5.5) has an architecture that separates the compute query engine from data storage. As a result, it is highly scalable at any amount of volume and concurrency. Pricing is based on the storage and compute used on a time-basis with their virtual databases instead of per bytes scanned. Tuning, indexes, and distribution keys aren't required for queries to be optimized and performant. Because of these reasons, it can be said that Snowflake has many of the benefits of both Redshift and Big Query.

Cons

Snowflake is a relatively new database in the market. Those familiar with SQL functions supported by databases like Redshift or PostgreSQL may find some inconsistencies in the SQL syntax for Snowflake. Snowflake is also generally more expensive.

Database Engines

For smaller amounts of data, less than 10GB, it's possible to use a transactional database for a data lake, but this limits the potential to scale in the future.

PostgreSQL

Pros

Unlike the options listed earlier, PostgreSQL (Figure 5.6) is an open source database that is free to download. It can easily be spun up

Figure 5.6

on a local server or hosted on various cloud services such as AWS. PostgreSQL also has an ANSI-compliant SQL library and supports an extensive library of third-party and user-defined functions. As it's a transactional database, it has very fast writes and also has fast reads below ~100M rows.

Cons

PostgreSQL is a straightforward, flexible solution that's different from Snowflake, Redshift, and BigQuery because it is a row-oriented database. This means it is more suited for processing transactional data over analytical queries. It's a single database connection not architected for parallel processing, so it generally doesn't perform as well with data volumes over 1TB. Consequently, PostgreSQL is great as a database, but is not a good choice for a data lake with a high volume data (>1TB). A lot of people do go this route though because they are very familiar with it and it is likely what their application is running on.

Recommendation

Selecting a data warehouse engine depends on several factors (Table 5.1). If short-term price and simplicity are the motivating factors, PostgreSQL may seem attractive; however, scalability potential is lower than columnar-based data warehouse solutions.

Redshift is a good choice as a standard cloud data warehouse when a dedicated DBA can manage it. BigQuery and Snowflake are both highly scalable solutions that don't require sophisticated management in contrast to Redshift. If concurrency limits are the driving

TABLE 5.1 Selection Factors

	Storage Pricing TB/Month	Process Pricing	Performance	Ecosystem	Maintenance
Redshift	Tiered/ Hourly	Variable/ Hourly	Columnar	AWS	Medium-high
BigQuery	$20	$5/TB	Columnar	GCP	Medium
Snowflake	$23	Dynamic/ hourly	Columnar	AWS/GCP/ Azure	Low
PostgreSQL	$0.115–0.125	$0.0180– 12.00/ hourly	Columnar and Row-Based	AWS/GCP/ Azure/Self	High

*   *Prices current as of April 2020. Redshift is priced based on region and service tiers, so while it is flexible, it's also more complex than other options.*
PostgreSQL pricing is based on AWS RDS service instance pricing. Competitors offer very similar offerings.

factors, then Snowflake or BigQuery are more suitable for your organization.

Remember, all of the data warehouse engines use the same C-Store architecture, so the differences in performance are not severe.

George Fraser CEO of Fivetran, a leader in software for extracting and loading data, summed up the decision process well in his annual warehouse-benchmark.

> *These warehouses all have excellent price and performance. We shouldn't be surprised that they are similar: The basic techniques for making a fast columnar data warehouse have been well-known since the C-Store paper was published in 2005. These data warehouses undoubtedly use the standard performance tricks: columnar storage, cost-based query planning, pipelined execution and just-in-time compilation. We should be skeptical of any benchmark claiming one data warehouse is orders of magnitude faster than another.*

The most important differences between warehouses are the qualitative differences caused by their design choices: Some warehouses emphasize tunability, others ease of use. If you're evaluating data warehouses, you should demo multiple systems, and choose the one that strikes the right balance for you.
                                        —George Fraser, CEO @ Fivetran

If you're the type of person who likes researching benchmarks, we recommend checking out Fivetran's excellent article, *Cloud Data Warehouse Benchmark: Redshift, Snowflake, Azure, Presto and BigQuery*, by George Fraser and Eric O'Connor: https://fivetran.com/blog/warehouse-benchmark.

Chapter Six

Extract and Load (EL) Data

So far, we've been outlining the practical aspects of what often is called Extract, Load, Transform (ELT) by modern data teams. The three letters refer to different stages of managing data, that is, the different steps for getting data from messy sources into polished information. In this stage, we focus on the first two letters. The third letter is covered in subsequent stages of the book.

For data to arrive in the data lake, data is *(E)xtracted* from its source, through SQL or an API, and then *(L)oaded* into the lake. This process is called *extract* and *load*—or "EL" for short. That data will also likely need further transformations that can make the data easier to query. There are many tools to help support this, but first, let's discuss an old debate: Should data be transformed before or after being loaded into a data lake?

ETL versus ELT

When in the extracting and loading process is it necessary to apply transformations to data? Well, there are two conventional paradigms for this (Figures 6.1 and 6.2).

1. E **T** L is the legacy method where transformations of data happen on the way to the lake. It arose in ecosystems with end-to-end data products.

2. E L **T** is the modern approach, where the transformation step happens after the data is loaded into the lake. The transformations occur when modeling the data in the data lake to make it into a data warehouse. It reflects a more modular approach to data analytics; different products representing different layers of the data stack are mixed and matched.

In the past data storage was expensive and it made sense to only put the cleaned important data in the warehouse. So there were extensive transform steps between the extract and load steps to filter and clean that data. This system was more complex, prone to error, and was less versatile when data needs changed. If for instance the transformation on a column changed, you would need

EXTRACT   **TRANSFORM**   **LOAD**

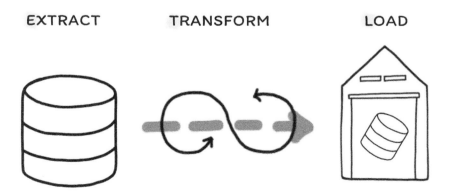

Figure 6.1 Data can be transformed while being moved to a data warehouse.

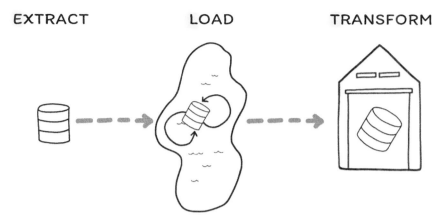

EXTRACT   **LOAD**   **TRANSFORM**

Figure 6.2 Data can first be loaded into a lake and transformed there. This transformed data is now the data warehouse.

to go all the way back to the source and re-import and re-transform all of that data again.

Now that storage is cheap we can do things a bit simpler. We first load all of the data with little or no transformation into the common lake. And then we do our transforms quite simply on top of it with simple SQL views or the equivalent. Now if a transform breaks or changes you don't have to go all the way back to the source and re-import the needed data. It's all already in the lake, you simply need to edit the SQL file that's doing the transform on top.

We recommend ELT because:

1. Extracting and loading the data to the data lake is the main priority at this stage.

2. Data in a lake goes through substantial transformations during the next stage, so there is no need for complex logic before the data is loaded.

3. We end up with a much simpler architecture, which means fewer problems and less maintenance.

4. Data lineage becomes more natural to track, as complex transformations are not happening before loading the data into the lake.

5. When your transformations or business logic need to change, there is no need to re-transport raw data from source systems of record into your own data source.

Light transformation of the data before loading the data into the lake might still be necessary:

- **Column selection:** Select the data that really matters. For example, not everything in Salesforce needs to be in the data lake.
- **Privacy reasons:** For example, filtering out columns that contain PII (personally identifiable information). Instead of filtering, consider hashing PII data so it can be safely used for analytics.

These transformation cases can be included in the ELT paradigm and are offered by most commercially available ELT vendors.

EL/ETL Vendors

There are a number of great modern EL vendors (sometimes called ELT vendors) such as Fivetran (Figure 6.3), Stitch Data (Figure 6.3), Matillion, Talend, Funnel, and Panopoly. There are also many other open source vendors in this space as well, such as Meltano and Airbyte.

EL providers build detailed extract scripts for the most popular APIs and offer a simple experience for extracting and loading data into data lakes. The process usually involves the setup of a pipeline where

Figure 6.3

both the destination and the data source are connected, then light data transformations are performed, for example, selecting what tables and fields to sync, hiding some values for privacy reasons.

Data loading with vendors requires minimal engineering effort in most cases (Figure 6.4).

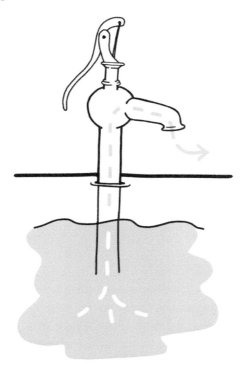

Figure 6.4

Extract Options

Extraction is the phase of pulling data out from a data source, through APIs or SQL. We can do a *complete extraction* of all data available, or we can do an *incremental extraction* every time we synchronize our data. A complete extraction extracts all the data from the data source. An incremental extraction only extracts updated records from the data source.

Complete Extraction

Complete extraction of data is the easiest way since no configuration is required, but it has three potentially significant disadvantages.

1. Historical data and state is lost.
   Imagine a row or field was deleted in a source. The next time we extract all data from our sources, we may lose historical context. Consider that an analyst looking at the source for the first time has no knowledge about what columns or rows used to exist. In addition, if fields contain slowly changing dimension fields (like a "status" or "type" field), you might override the old values in place and no longer have a record of what the business logic used to be.

2. Duplicate data ends up in the data lake.
   It can make sense to keep existing extractions of the data when a complete extraction is done so that you can find data that was deleted or previous values of slowly changing dimensions. This can result in a lot of extra data. While data is relatively cheap to store and compute, this can become problematic to load and store as the amount of data scales.

3. The complexity of the next steps in the analytics stack increases.
   Sometimes taking all the data "as-is" means creating more work later on to make sense of it. One caveat when considering a full extraction is that some columns and tables may not prove to be very useful for analysis. In stages beyond the data lake, we'll be focused on cleaning data. This involves removing extraneous columns. By taking in all columns now with a complete extraction, you may be making things more complicated.

Incremental Extraction

The preferred alternative is to do incremental extractions. Incremental extractions are challenging due to the need to check for new or updated rows and account for changing schemas. However, it is typically preferred because much less data is processed, requiring fewer updates to the data lake. All cloud ELT vendors support incremental extractions from data sources.

The main downside to incremental extraction is deletions in a data source, which are not easy to detect. This is because it would need to scan the entire database and have saved snapshots of the history. How does anyone know something is missing if there is no record of it? ELT providers do not guarantee consistency under deletions in most cases; in some cases, it's possible or implemented by the source, for example, data is never deleted but flagged as "is_deleted" instead.

A complete dump would guarantee always having a replica of the source state (Figure 6.5). Keep in mind that in analytics this is not typically that useful, but keeping the deleted records might be required for other reasons such as compliance.

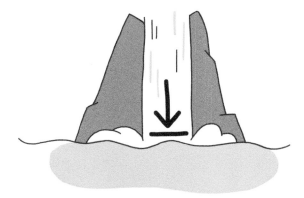

Figure 6.5

Load Options

However the data is extracted from its source, there are multiple ways to store it in a database. Push changes through to existing data in the data lake or store this new data separate from existing data.

Push Changes

When using a database system as a data lake, the updates to the data can be loaded and pushed into the existing schema. This will end up having a close replica of the data from the source system to the data lake, and it optimizes storage.

Store Separate

Another option is saving changes without updating the records. Saving changes separately when using a file system data source avoids adding complexity to the data lake. The benefit of storing changes separately is that there's a history of how data has changed.

Multiple Schemas

Most EL vendors insert each source into the lake as a new schema (Figure 6.6). The organization of schema by source eliminates the chance of commonly named tables overwriting each other.

When querying between schemas, it's only necessary to remember to specify the schema names in addition to the table names. For example, we could combine Salesforce user data with Zendesk user data:

```
SELECT
  *
FROM
  salesforce.user AS sf_user
JOIN
  zendesk.user as zd_user
ON
  sf_user.email == zd_user.email
```

Figure 6.6

This can be useful for a query to figure out what size companies have the most number of tickets. Combining sources like this will become a best practice, which we will cover in Stage 3: Data Warehouse.

Other Extract and Load Routes

Traditional ETL

For the reasons we've outlined here, we recommend ELT over ETL. If traditional means of ETL are necessary, with transformations happening before things are loaded into the lake, there are products that help support it such as Xplenty or Amazon Glue. There are also open source tools such as Airflow which many people use to orchestrate their data pipelines.

 Apache Airflow

Apache Airflow is a popular open-source project that allows developers to create custom workflows that commonly involve data transformations and other types of ETL tasks.

Using traditional approaches skips over the lake stage and goes straight to a data warehouse. This makes data transformations difficult to keep track of and update as needed. Without some kind of structure to keep things organized, it's unclear what queries are doubling up the work of others. At best, you go digging through code snippets and ad-hoc SQL files to figure out what certain translations are trying to accomplish. In the long run, we've found that this ends up costing more money than saved initially.

DIY

When building a data lake, it may be tempting to implement a custom solution for loading the data to it. There are a number of maintenance costs to keep in mind:

- Slowing other projects down.
- Updating code whenever data changes.

- Updating code for new BI requirements.
- Exponential complexity as the number of data sources increase.
- Exponential complexity to confirm data integrity as data grows.
- Having to keep track of end-to-end scripts (e.g. so-called transformation pipelines).
- Managing the infrastructure to support all of the above.

Generally, extract and load projects start simple but then require quite a bit of effort to maintain long term as data grows in complexity. The biggest reason DIY is generally a wrong choice is that extracting and loading costs more when data scientists, analysts, and engineers do it rather than a third-party service provider. The cost of extracting and loading data in this day and age is now cheaper than it ever has been, and it makes sense to use services like Stitch, Fivetran, and so on as much as possible.

However, building a custom extract and load solution in-house makes sense when:

- The data source is not supported.
- The EL service level agreement isn't comprehensive enough.
- Business requirements are not met by third-party tools.

While implementation is possible with DIY pipelines and useful in the scenarios above, using a vendor saves a lot of time and money. Using a provider to extract and load data is simpler to maintain, and it also allows data professionals to work on more valuable tasks.

Chapter Seven

Data Lake Security

Besides making data querying easier, data lakes in fact lead to better security outcomes. Without a unified data store, all analysis occurs in many different places. These far-flung data sources require individual logins, which are hard to track and maintain the appropriate levels of access. It's unclear who has access to what. It can be hard to redact sensitive information that should not be used in company analytics. In other words, different sources of data are hard to manage.

With all the data in one spot and in one common engine, a data lake makes managing permissions much simpler. Common warehouse solutions come with power IAM management tools in addition to ordinary database security features.

Likewise, data coming into the data lake is likely not yet clean, so sensitive information may still exist. A data lake gives your security specialists fine control over what data can and cannot be accessed.

Avoid extracting or loading sensitive data/columns; instead, configure these items within the ELT tools. Also, be mindful of who can access the data lake since more data is accessible than individual data sources initially.

Access in Central Place

To simplify the management of access across multiple data sources, we recommend removing access from specific tools (such as BI), then migrating all access management to the data lake. Limiting access from multiple sources to one lake cuts down on access requests and mishaps where people retain access to information they shouldn't have. You can then provide BI tool access to this new singular source (Figure 7.1).

Figure 7.1 Security moves from each data source to the data lake.

Permission Tiers

Now that the data is in one place, granting general permission is simple. However, specific controls should be put into place for different groups to make sure users are not seeing data they shouldn't.

Start out by creating two user groups on the data lake as follows:

1. For admin and engineers (Full Access)

2. For analysts and business users (Relevant Access)

It's possible to prevent the second group from accessing sensitive data in the data lake by limiting that group's permissions to only relevant schemas or tables. We only encourage limiting data access based on sensitivity; other limitations may artificially restrict questions and prevent insights from being found.

In Figure 7.2 we see engineering maintaining access to all schemas and marketing and success sharing almost all schemas except Salesforce, which may have sensitive data about potential customers or compensation.

In general, set broad controls for ease of management. As a company grows in data sophistication and transitions to progressive stages, it's easier to create more and more refined permission settings.

	MARKETING	ENGINEERING	SUCCESS
Chartio Analytics	✓	✓	✓
Financials		✓	
Hubspot Stitch	✓	✓	✓
Fivetran Salesforce		✓	✓
Fivetran Marketo (Deprecated)		✓	

Figure 7.2 A table of data sources and with a key graphic indicating which company department needs access.

Chapter Eight

Data Lake Maintenance

Initially, data lakes will not be well organized or maintained with a broader audience in mind. When first loading data sources to a data lake, their structure is pretty much the same as before they ended up in the lake (Figure 8.1). These structures can be hard to understand and query; however, they do not need to be cleaned up too much yet. The majority of the cleaning will take place in creating the data warehouse.

The areas of focus for data lake maintenance are around:

- SQL
- Extracting and loading of data sources
- Performance

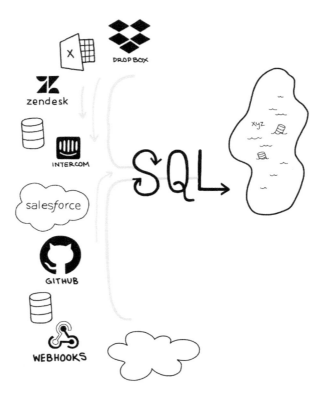

Figure 8.1 Source data being loaded with SQL into a data lake.

These maintenance activities can be expensive once data is extracted and loaded with custom scripts. It's necessary to have in-depth knowledge of the data, such as where data originates, the details of the APIs, and the data structures inside it. Also, the potential need to write new code and maintain existing code when data sources update is high. We recommend avoiding manual extract and load; use tools like Fivetran or Stitch, which automatically handle data source updates so that any data engineers can focus on more critical tasks.

Why SQL?

While the data could be loaded into the lake in a variety of formats, we recommend SQL (Figure 8.1). It's the standard language for relational database management systems (which is what a Data Warehouse is built on) and it's the ideal environment for the data lake. Working in an SQL-based model is ideal for a number of reasons:

- A variety of tools and platforms support SQL.
- SQL can be put in version control systems for team collaboration.
- The vast majority of data professionals and some business users are proficient with SQL.
- SQL simplifies the management and integration of the warehouse.

Data Sources

The main place where maintenance issues occur is when the data from the sources changes or the data is not making it from the source into the data lake (Figure 8.2).

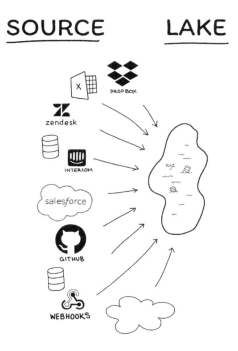

Figure 8.2 More sources being added to the data lake.

Adding New Data Sources

Ideally, this is as simple as clicking a few buttons inside of an ELT product. Products such as Fivetran and Stitch have large numbers of connectors for different data sources (Figure 8.3).

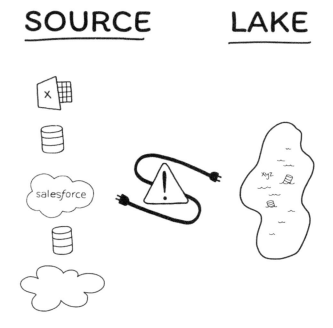

Figure 8.3 Data sources having errors connecting to the data lake.

Data Source Updates

Sources change all the time, and ELT tools manage these changes. The purpose of ELT is to move data from data sources to other data stores, so when an API updates its format, these types of ELT tools ensure the right data is still moved to the right place.

Fixing Broken Connections

Occasionally, it's necessary to reconfigure some source queries manually. For example, when a data source adds a new field or removes a specific table, some of the queries that BI tools depend on might break (Figure 8.4). This is frustrating but it very well may be unavoidable to track down broken queries and update them to work with a new version of the API.

For instance, someone may change a field name in Salesforce, let's say arr (annual recurring revenue) to arr_dollars. We may have a query like this on our dashboard that would break:

```
SELECT
    SUM(arr)
FROM
    salesforce.leads
```

We need to update the field name in the query to be in line with the data source.

```
SELECT
    SUM(arr_dollars)
FROM
    Salesforce.leads
```

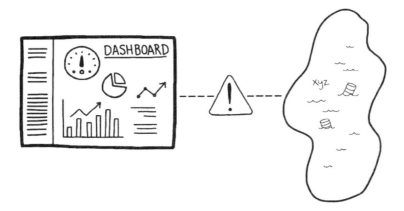

Figure 8.4 A warning about the connection to the data lake.

Each BI product has a different way of handling these migrations. Rather than worrying about how that data is being processed and visualized, a data lake–powered team only has to worry about loading that information forward—a much more addressable issue.

Performance

When it comes to optimization, at the data lake stage of agile data organization, it's most practical to focus attention on the dashboard or query level.

Optimize Individual Queries

There are simple concepts to keep in mind when optimizing queries. The strategies that have the most impact on query performance include:

- Only joining in what columns are necessary.
- Select only the required columns for analysis.

 Book Recommendation

We want to teach you everything about SQL optimization, but that's a bit off-topic. We recommend the online book *Optimizing SQL* by Matt David:

https://dataschool.com/sql-optimization/.

Caching

Many BI products allow caching data to improve query speeds; this reduces strain on the database (Figure 8.5). It moves queries from hitting the database directly to a faster data store. Caching allows queries to use the faster data store multiple times without performance loss. The only downside of caching is that it reduces the real-time nature of analytical queries; the queries hit the data store and not the live data. Until the cache is updated, the data is not live.

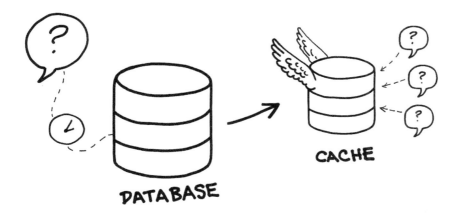

Figure 8.5 A database receiving a query, then fetching data from a cached store.

Create Limits

Some platforms struggle with concurrency, where lots of people are querying the same source at once. Improve query speed in these scenarios by limiting how many queries people can perform on the database. While this can be a blow to people's curiosity or analysis, it quickly solves this performance problem (Figure 8.6).

Queries can be limited in different ways:

- Limit number of people querying.
- Limit queries per day.
- Big Query—Set max bytes (Figure 8.7).

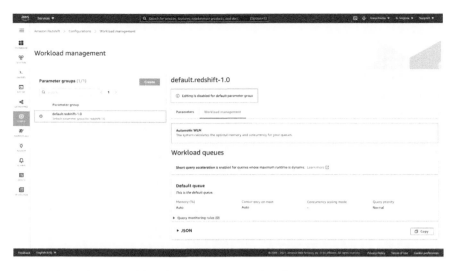

Figure 8.6 The "Workload Management Configuration" section on an AWS Redshift Dashboard.
Source: Amazon.com, Inc.

Destination Table	Select Table	No table selected	
Write Preference	● Write if empty	○ Append to table	○ Overwrite table
Results Size	☐ Allow Large Results (?)		
Results Schema	☑ Flatten Results (?)		
Query Caching	☑ Use Cached Results (?)		
Query Priority	● Interatcive	○ Batch (?)	
UDF Source URIs	Edit (?)		
Maximum Billing Tier	Project Default (?)		
Maximum Bytes Billed	1000000 (?)		
SQL Dialect	☐ Use Legacy SQL (?)		

RUN QUERY ▼   Save Query   Save view   Format Query   Hide Options

Figure 8.7 In Google Cloud's BigQuery, it's possible to set maximum bytes billed as a threshold to limit query resource utilization.
Source: Google LLC

Scheduling

Examine how BI products query the database. Does it schedule when queries run automatically or is it a manual process? Products such as Chartio have options to schedule queries to run at off-peak times to balance the load on the database and have types of "smart refresh" options to prevent queries from running when dashboards aren't actively being viewed (Figure 8.8).

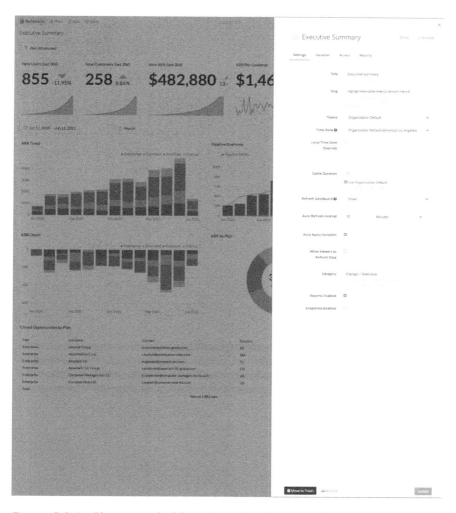

Figure 8.8 In Chartio, a dashboard setting for controlling the frequency of fetching results.
Source: CHARTIO

These sorts of tweaks become especially important as more users query the database.

Upgrade Snippets to Views

Snippets were a useful way to write queries more quickly against the database. The database though has the capability to store a full query and return the output table as a table you and others can query directly from. This is called a view (more on views in the next section). Begin making some views to assist analysis such as wider tables that contain more categorical information to make segmenting data easier. These should be one-off ad-hoc views at this point. Eventually you will want to build a layer of views on top of your lake to create an entire schema or schemas that are easier to use by everyone in your company to query and analyze.

STAGE 3
DATA WAREHOUSE
aka the Single Source of Truth

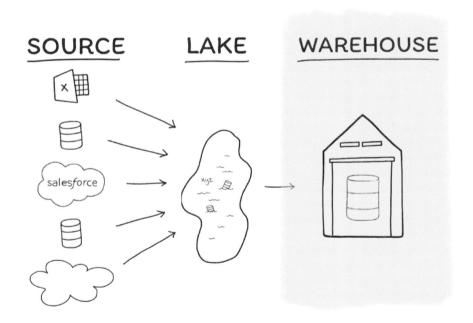

Warehouse Stage Overview

The data warehouse is created by layering views on top of your data lake in order to make the data easier for everyone to use and understand. This is a powerful abstraction that makes it manageable to deal with the growing and changing data sources that your business relies upon. Let's first imagine the best-case scenario of what a data warehouse would look like as part of a data stack.

ZenHubInterAppForceDB

Imagine a single, comprehensive, and organized database runs your company's integrated suite of production and third-party SaaS applications. The data is clearly labeled, and it has been organized in a way that makes querying and exploration simple, not just for you but really anyone on the team. There is no duplicate information, silos, or zombie data, the tables that no longer have a purpose but keep hanging around. All of your applications work on it.

We sometimes call this dream system ZenHubInterAppForceDB (Figure P.1), as it would contain and do everything that all of those applications could.

Unfortunately, this ideal is impractical today. Companies run on dozens or even hundreds of different applications, each with their own data structures storing information that often needs to be tied together from different places, stored in different formats, and accessed through different APIs or languages.

While the ideal ZenHubInterAppForceDB does not exist, joining data and modeling it on top of our data lake can get us data that looks like it! We can create it iteratively through layering views on top of the data lake. As we model the data, the single source of truth emerges.

Instead of having data from different platforms smushed together into haphazard schemas that comprise a data lake, this single source

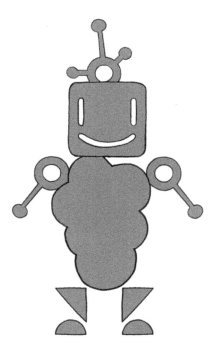

Figure P.1

of truth, carefully sanitized, combined, and transformed, scrubs away the inconsistencies in disparate source tables (Figure P.2). The single source of truth is an easy-to-query set of tables that encode business logic. And it is this that a company calls their data warehouse (or single source of truth, commonly abbreviated as SST).

In a single source of truth, data has already been cleaned and organized, which is more accessible both to the company analysts and the rest of your team. A cutting-edge warehouse empowers everyone from data pros to data-adjacent stakeholders to query more quickly and confidently and with fewer mistakes. Data transformations are permanent and represented in code, so that they are visible to anyone interested. Among other benefits, your data team will be able to train new people faster, work more effectively, make

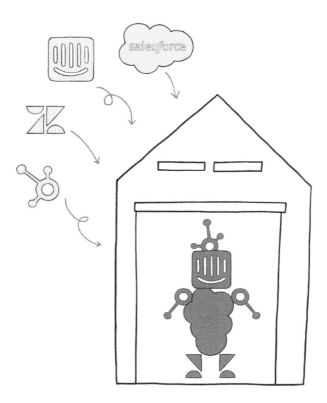

Figure P.2

fewer mistakes, and even involve more business users to explore the data themselves, that is, to self-serve answers to more of their questions.

Agile Warehouse Building with Layers

In the data lake stage, we extracted and loaded the data sources of your company into one place, so that all data could be queried wholesale in one language. This is a fantastic start that should have caused a few headaches to disappear already. But, source data grows on and on, and in time, it becomes common to get lost in schemas and tables in the data lake. Not only are there more tables and records to manage, the data itself is still incredibly messy, as it's in a raw form: the data piped into a lake from sources has not been cleaned or assembled together in any particular way.

In this data warehouse stage, we add layers of views on top of the data lake. These views create a cleaned and integrated set of schemas that serve as your data warehouse/single source of truth. It brings order back to a chaotic-looking landscape and makes your data much simpler to query and analyze. The best part of this layering approach is that it can begin with a single table.

Cleaning a single table helps people use that data immediately and get value out of it. As you clean more tables, it becomes easier for everyone to use more of the database. Then you can combine tables and link them to create a data warehouse. We split these modeling activities into two categories: staging for cleaning, and SST for combining and linking (Figure P.3).

In this section, we'll discuss end-to-end warehouse development, beginning with cleaning a single table to make staging view and ending with managing access to the data warehouse that you've implemented. Along the way, we touch on our favorite methods of structuring data into schemas supported by software engineering principles. Our favorite tool for transforming data, the data build tool (dbt), plays a special role in this leg of the journey.

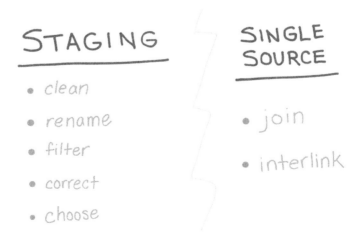

STAGING
- clean
- rename
- filter
- correct
- choose

SINGLE SOURCE
- join
- interlink

Figure P.3

Chapter Nine

The Power of Layers and Views

Your data in the data lake is stored as tables; we will transform them using views to first create staging schemas and then the warehouse, and we can then materialize those views to increase performance. First, let's clarify the difference between views tables and materialized views.

A *table* is physically stored and only updated when new data is loaded into the lake or if the schema is changed.

A *view* is a saved query that returns a table that can then be queried (Figure 9.1). The table it returns is not physically stored. The view will reflect any changes in the underlying data it is querying.

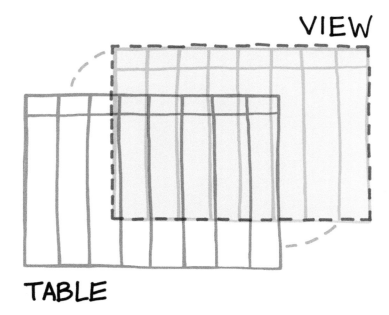

VIEW

TABLE

Figure 9.1 A view references a table's data without changing how the table's data is stored.

A *materialized view* is physically stored, and is updated whenever an upstream table or view is updated.

To build the staging schema and the data warehouse, default to using SQL views. Views work essentially the same as tables. Using views helps prevent storing additional data and incurring extra cost overhead, with few exceptions. There are usually no significant performance gains from creating new tables or materializing every view as part of your transformations to build a data warehouse; there are a few exceptions, which we will touch on later in this section. Lastly, views are non-destructive to the original data, so there's no need to worry about committing to changes that render the data less flexible.

Views allow us to quickly transform data without needing to build new structures within the warehouse. Anytime we use the term *view*, it could be materialized if needed for your database performance.

Make Readable Views

In a data lake, the schema reflects the transactional logic of an application and follows best practices (such as the third normal form) so that updating values don't produce errors. The data lake schema can be difficult to navigate because table conventions are inconsistent and there are many tables not needed for analysis within the schema.

 Third Normal Form (3NF) and Normalized data

Standards of database structures that minimize redundancies with data integrity in mind are described by 11 principles sometimes called "normal forms." The more you minimize the redundancies the more you normalize the data. Most databases are built in third normal form, which says that each row in a table must be able to be uniquely identified, given the values of columns that describe a row. When data cannot follow the third normal form, it's better to break it up into more tables.

Traditional books recommend using dimensional modeling to create star schemas to make tables easier to use for analysis and to enhance performance. However, due to advances in BI tools and other data warehouse technologies, dimensional modeling is no longer the only or maybe even the best way because visualization products now support querying more complex schemas (Figure 9.2).

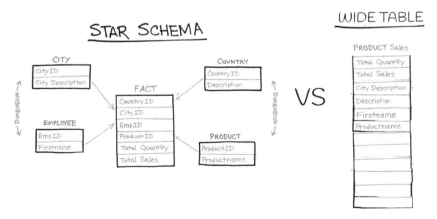

Figure 9.2 A view is an SQL abstraction on top of underlying data.

With the advent of modern warehouse engines, the performance benefits of using star schema for marts no longer exist. They are a significant amount of work to implement, and the usability benefits can be achieved through creating wide tables that are just as easy to understand. In fact, according to Michael Kaminsky in a guest post on Fivetran's blog, wide tables actually outperform star schema. Keep your data in the same format as your data warehouse and occasionally make wide tables when needed.

As we create these wider tables for the data warehouse, we should also look to exclude tables and columns that represent app-specific logic that isn't needed for analysis. We want the warehouse to not only be readable but easy to navigate. A great way to ensure that each addition to the warehouse is useful is to build the warehouse in pieces.

Layer Views on Views

Since a view produces a table from which we can query, we can create a view on top of a view (Figure 9.3). We first put a layer down to clean the tables from our data sources. This allows us to handle data source changes elegantly because the data sources are not directly being queried by the warehouse; we can change what things are referred to in these staging schemas and pass the new fields into warehouse views.

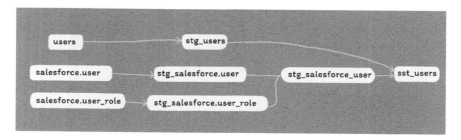

Figure 9.3 Views can reference other views allowing you to create layers within your warehouse.

We can start by cleaning one table at a time and providing that to analysts and other business users. Then, we can begin joining these staging schemas together to create a warehouse that should be much easier to navigate.

The process laid out does not have to be a straight line between two points (sources and an SST). Sometimes, the right strategy involves fashioning staging schemas (covered soon) more on the fly and tending to them as separate structures in your lake. After gaining some experience with your data models, you could work to combine them into a single source of truth.

Why is this a good alternative to aiming for a unified SST immediately? Staging schemas alone are a huge value add, as their goal is to organize and standardize data for maximum clarity. One step in this process is renaming columns to more easily understood names. With staging schemas, fewer members of your organization need to remember what obscure columns like c_1, c_2, c_3 in your crm.users table mean.

Modeling data decreases the necessary background knowledge your company must have to write queries of their own. This in turn lowers the barrier to data literacy across your organization, and as we argued at the outset, a more informed team is a more effective one.

If taking on the entire problem at once seems daunting, we still encourage you to jump in and get started with one table. We think you'll pick it up quickly and find data modeling to be among the most impactful things anyone can do for a company's success. It sure doesn't hurt that this process can be a great deal of fun.

Before we dive into the technical details, we'd like to offer perspective derived from working with several past companies working to move from data lake to date warehouse. We've seen several teams struggle to move past the data lake. Cardinal sin number one is that teams often misjudge how long and how much work building a data warehouse takes. They believe that the entire thing must be architected ahead of modeling and that it must be completed as part of a single project.

This is not true; you do not have to build it all at once. We can continue to add layers of views on top of the data lake, making the data clean and more useful. Eventually the final layers will be the SST. This can be done incrementally one view and layer at a time. This also helps you stay organized and helps you avoid repetition.

Here's a word of reassurance before we begin. The anxiety or hesitation project leads often feel when scoping out the problem is understandable (Figure 9.4). There's a lot of advice out there, but some of it conflicts and rests on one-off blog posts. Meanwhile, books like *Dimensional Modeling* aim for completeness and technical precision at the price of practical comprehensibility (not to mention these were written largely before the current Cloud warehousing revolution). Plenty of well-equipped data professionals struggle to decide how to design and implement a data warehouse. We have even seen project leads overestimate implementation time in an attempt to hedge their position. Their estimated timelines? Development timescales on the order of months or even years!

That said, we relate to how unclear it can be to set up a warehouse for the first time. The good news is that, like all problems in the engineering world, it can be broken down into steps and design principles, and can be tackled iteratively.

Figure 9.4 It may not be obvious at first how to model data, start with making one table easier to use.

Start with a Single View

Starting by cleaning a single table is very doable; before you know it, you will have cleaned several. These sub-problems are solvable with common sense design and a familiarity with SQL. We intend to touch on the major mechanics that you'll need to tackle those challenges (Figure 9.5).

Figure 9.5 A warehouse is a cleaned usable version of the data in the lake.

We need an individual to begin this process whom we dub the warehouse lead; if you are reading this book, you may be one of them. Creating an effective data warehouse involves ongoing iteration and feedback. For that reason, we not only discuss how to build a warehouse but also the responsibilities involved with managing a warehouse.

Chapter Ten

Staging Schemas

Before building the single source of truth, we recommend first making idealized versions of each of the sources in the data lake. These are called staging schemas (Figure 10.1).

Generally, a staging schema holds models (i.e. tables or views) that handle transformations of this type. The tables and columns that are unneeded or empty are removed, weird names are improved, and unwanted data is filtered out. The value of investing time into cleaning and renaming data fields lies in making the data ready for more complex numeric transformations without needing to worry about these sorts of consistencies. Some may be concerned about the space implications from having many staging tables or repeated data. The good news, however, is that the compression strategies of a modern C-Store warehouse handle exactly this kind of data organization without noticeable performance hits.

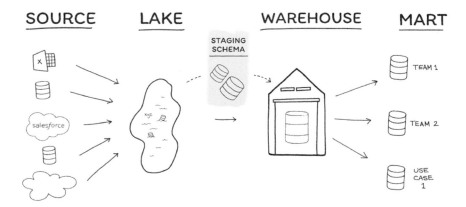

SOURCE   LAKE   WAREHOUSE   MART

STAGING
SCHEMA

TEAM 1

TEAM 2

USE
CASE
1

Figure 10.1 The four stages of agile data organization with an intermediary step that illustrates where a "staging schema" is relevant.

Here's a last note on process: as each source is cleaned, it never hurts to give read-only access to departments across your organization. Showing the value of the modeling and asking for feedback during creation are ways your team can earn trust and confidence from stakeholders.

Orient to the Schemas

Go through the list of tables in the schemas and find ones that speak to the use case that has been identified. Identify tables that have any relevant columns even if it is only one. We have seen companies send out surveys to stakeholders to identify relevant tables, and we have seen companies where the warehouse lead makes the calls. This can be done iteratively; we can always add more tables or remove tables from the staging schema (Figure 10.2).

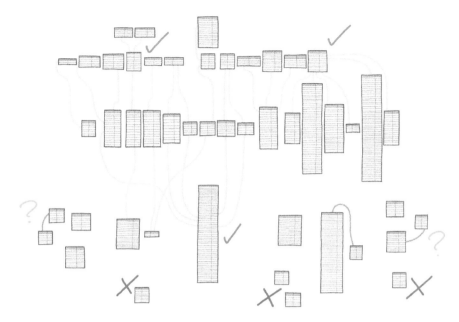

Figure 10.2

Pick a Table and Clean It

Let's explore different straightforward tools for making tables staging-schema-ready. These techniques should be applied to whichever subset of your sources needs cleaning. Which sources should have a staging model? Whichever will be used in the warehouse, even if the purpose of a staging model is to provide information to another staging table.

First, start with one of your more important but also simple tables. We want our first modeling effort to be valuable but not too difficult. (A users table can be a good place to start.)

Let's take an example source users table in a data lake and explore the issues with it and how we would correct them using SQL (Figure 10.3).

Users							
Id	External_Id	Name	Display Name	Location	Type	Info	is_deleted

21590	68791	Doug Gonzalez	D Gonzalez	United States	1	{
						  groups: ["Admin", "R&D"]
						  title: "Director of R&D",
						  status: "active"
						}
							False

13107	32699	NULL	Sales	USA	3	{
						  groups: "Sales"
						  title: "",
						  status: "active"
						}
							True

29448	28175	Josh	Josh Redman	US	2	{
						  groups: ["Marketing", "HR"]
						  title: "CMO",
						  status: "inactive"
						}
							False

32641	19873	Hannah To	NULL	US of A	1	{
						  groups: ["Sales", "Editor"]
						  title: "Account Executive",
						  status: "active"
						}
							False

Figure 10.3

Starting from left to right:

1. Having multiple Id columns can be confusing.

2. NULLs can produce unexpected results during aggregations.

3. Unclear naming makes it hard for people to know which column to use.

4. Inconsistent values make it hard to aggregate and group the data accurately.

5. Numeric categories are hard to interpret; they require the analyst to ask an engineer for clarification.

6. Parsing JSON sucks. Would you rather do it once or every time you have to query this table?

7. Analysts often miss deprecated data flags, so this leaves room for error in aggregations.

Let's mark up the chart visually to make it more clear (Figure 10.4).

To address these issues, keep the analyst/business user in mind and make all of the fields easy for them to interpret.

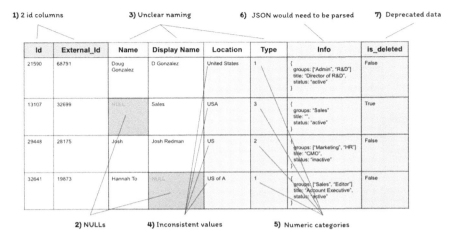

Figure 10.4

Eliminate Columns

There are many reasons for seemingly unusable columns; in this case we have an External_Id field that could be used to JOIN data. The purpose of certain fields is not always clear to analysts. Since there is already an Id column, and we're unclear what External_Id means or what it should be used for, we can remove the External_Id column by commenting it out:

```
SELECT
  Id,
  -- external_id, -- unused
  Name,
  Display Name,
  Location,
  Type,
  Info,
  is_deleted
FROM
  app.users
```

Later in the book we will show why this removal might have been an error and how to correct it.

For potentially confusing removals add an inline comment in the query like above. If later down the line someone shows why they do need this column, you can simply un-comment it and bring it into the model again. In some organizations they prefer to remove any unused code, so removing it completely from the query can work as well.

 SQL IDEs for modeling

Many SQL IDEs like DataGrip help you turn SELECT * queries into this more verbose query with all the columns explicitly listed out. This can save a bunch of time writing views for your Data Warehouse and Data Mart.

Even if we were keeping the entire table, instead of writing a SELECT * FROM [tablename] query, we should write out all the columns that should be kept. This will make it easier to edit in the future and prevent new columns from being added in without us knowing.

Ensure Table and Column Names Are Understandable

Transactional schemas often have weird names that make sense to the engineer who built the original schema, but there's no guarantee that knowledge will translate to you, the data team as a whole, or other departments in the company who want to self-serve data insights. One technique for supporting intercompany knowledge exchange is renaming tables and columns so that anyone, even folks new to the data, can have a reasonable chance of interpreting it correctly.

To rename a column, put the AS keyword after the column name in the query and then put the desired name. If the desired name has a space in it, you will need to put it in quotes. Quoting rules can differ from warehouse engine to warehouse engine. We use snake case, only lowercase letters and putting an underscore where spaces would be, by default to sidestep naming troubles:

```
bad_column_name AS better_column_name
```

This is called aliasing in SQL. You can also just place the desired name after the column; it is a stylistic choice but can make it less clear what is going on. From the example, in our select statement above, it is hard to know what the "Type" field indicates. We can remove this uncertainty with aliasing:

```
SELECT
  Id,
  -- external_id, -- unused
  Name,
  Display Name,
  Location,
  Type AS Access_level,
  Info,
  is_deleted
FROM
  app.users
```

Now the column name is more explicit, but the values themselves are still hard to interpret.

Ensure Values Are Readable

Data fields often encode statuses of orders, user activity, and so much more, but so many little numbers or abbreviations become difficult to manage. To make values clear, spell out status codes, days of week, and other numeric categories and abbreviations.

For example, a column "day_of_week" which stores a numeric value for the day of the week (1 is Sunday, 2 is Monday) is not as easy to read if you just replaced the numbers with names of the week themselves. Also, many times developers will use 0-based indexing, which might mean Sunday is 0 and Monday would be 1, so check to make sure how the encoding works before re-labeling the data. Better to figure this out once than every time you run a query and have to explain the results to someone (or have to figure it out for yourself).

We'll illustrate this by continuing from the previous example. Suppose the values of the Type column are a set of integers one through three that each stands for some level of access level to an asset within the application this data is sourced from. This might need to be figured out by consulting the stakeholder for this data source. Turn numbers into descriptive names using a CASE statement:

```
SELECT
  id,
  -- external_id, -- unused
  Name,
  Display Name,
  Location,
  CASE
        WHEN Type = "1" THEN "Can view"
        WHEN Type = "2" THEN "Can edit"
        WHEN Type = "3" THEN "Can admin"
        END AS access_level,
  Info,
  is_deleted
FROM
  app.Users
```

However, we can go a step further. Numeric categories are quite often foreign keys to a reference table with more explicit data (Figure 10.5). If those lookup tables are available, you can JOIN in their more explicit values instead. This reduces querying complexity for end users and makes fields straightforward to interpret.

This alternative strategy joins two tables on the mutually shared type column. The lookup table version of the type value is kept in the query, whereas the id is commented out or omitted. In the interest of having straightforward names, the type column from the Access table may be renamed to access_level.

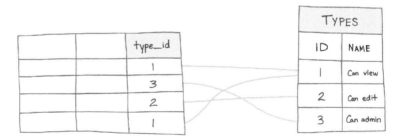

Figure 10.5

```
SELECT
  id,
  -- external_id, -- unused
  Name,
  Display Name,
  Location,
  access."type" AS access_level,
  --type --replaced by access_level
  Info,
  is_deleted
FROM
  app.Users
JOIN
  app.access
ON
  Users.type = access.id
```

If you have the table with spelled out values, use the JOIN approach. Using case statements requires hard-coding data values in your queries. What happens if a backend change causes a value to change? What if a new key-value is added to the field? This takes a lot of upkeep. The JOIN strategy minimizes this overhead.

Standardize Values

Sometimes, column values are human readable but their individual level of granularity differs across the column. For example, say that some rows in an order table have a price given in US dollars while others have a price given in euros. This would make it difficult to do a simple aggregation of the column. All sorts of difficulties like this complicate analysis.

Take a peek back to that query we've been working on. One of the fields SELECT-ed is the location field. Suppose we expect to see only nation-level values, but instead there are some rows with state-level values. We can fix this inconsistent data, again, with CASE statements:

```
SELECT
  id,
  -- external_id, -- unused
  Name,
  Display Name,
  CASE
            WHEN Location = "United States" THEN "USA"
            WHEN Location = "US" THEN "USA"
            WHEN Location = "US of A" THEN "USA"
            ELSE Location
  END AS country,
  access."type" AS access_level,
  --type --replaced by access_level
  Info,
  is_deleted
FROM
  app.Users
JOIN
  app.access
ON
  Users.type = access.id
```

For long or cumbersome CASE statements, consider factoring them out into separate CTEs. Breaking up large queries into discrete chunks helps to make analysis more manageable in general. CTEs can also be handled more programmatically with modeling tools, which we will cover in the next chapter.

 Common Table Expressions (WITH statements)

Common Table Expressions, or CTEs, are queries that run prior to the main query that produce a table of data that other queries in the same file can access. They operate in the same way as sub-queries but are often easier to read and maintain. These are begun with the WITH keyword, a name for the CTE, and the AS keyword.

Extract Fields from Structured Columns (JSON)

Another common query hurdle arises from the format of the data itself. For example, data is often stored as JSON, which is fairly readable due to its hierarchical structure, especially to machines.

In our example, the Info column contains structured data. One record has this value for its Info field:

```
{
  groups: ["Admin","R&D"],
  title: "Director of R&D",
  status: "active"
};
```

Only the subfield status happens to hold any significance to your analysis. Here's the bad news: SQL was not originally designed to interface directly with JSON, and some database management systems *continue* to lack "native" support for handling structured data. Additional processing is required either using regexes or helper scripts. This is a reminder that part of selecting the right warehouse engine is knowing which one has the toolset you need for your analysis.

Extract Data Using Wildcards

Sometimes data is formatted consistently (or semi-consistently) within a column, but the values themselves are still not in a ready-to-use format. This can happen especially when the values in a column are set automatically by (automated) application code. Often, junk characters complicate fields. Using CASE statements and a wildcard or two can help you clean up or modify those values. Let's apply wildcards to extract the status from the info field. Since we know what the two status types are, we can search for those directly:

```
SELECT
  id,
  -- external_id, -- unused
  Name,
  Display Name,
  CASE
          WHEN Location = "United States" THEN "USA"
          WHEN Location = "US" THEN "USA"
          WHEN Location = "US of A" THEN "USA"
          ELSE Location
  END AS country,
  access."type" AS access_level,
  --type --replaced by access_level
  CASE
          WHEN Info = "%active" THEN True
          WHEN Info = "%inactive" THEN False
  END AS is_active,
  is_deleted
FROM
  app.Users
JOIN
  app.access
ON
  Users.type = access.id
```

 Wildcards

Wildcards allow you to search and locate specific sequences of characters that match a pattern. Wildcards let you define a pattern using comparators and metacharacters. The most commonly used metacharacter is %, which means it will match any string. So in the example above %active will match with a value that ends with active such as 123active, ABCactive, and even just active.

Decide What to Do about Null Fields

Unstructured data often have NULL values. Well, technically NULL isn't a value. In the SQL specification, NULL is defined as the *absence* of a value. In other words, SQL engines do not tend to enforce that there be a value for each field in every column. Our task, as data professionals, is to figure out how to handle these blank/empty/nonexistent values. Why would this happen at all?

Consider a new user who has not completed their profile information. For instance, they have not entered their first and last name. They surely have a name, though, so we leave the field NULL in the database. However, there are cases where NULLs may be produced by accident or they may need to be replaced with a value. For each column that could have NULLs, it's a good idea to determine what those mean and correct NULLs with CASE-WHEN statements if there should never be a blank value in reports.

Filter Unwanted Rows

Occasionally rows will be marked as deprecated or were created for test purposes. Instead of asking everyone to filter these out in their queries, it is a best practice to filter them out in staging tables using WHERE clauses and Boolean expressions (i.e. expressions that produce a true or false value).

Rows may have "Boolean flags" (columns that can only be true or false). These are often phrased as predicates, such as "is_active" or "is_deleted." Why would you need an "is_deleted" field? Sometimes, records are effectively removed from applications but not outright deleted. Either they are kept around for historical analysis or, say, in case if a customer who requires an account deletion has second thoughts before the record is fully erased. In the meantime, flag fields can help sort out effectively "dead" records from analyses:

```
SELECT
  id,
  -- external_id, -- unused
  Name,
  Display Name,
  CASE
          WHEN Location = "United States" THEN "USA"
          WHEN Location = "US" THEN "USA"
          WHEN Location = "US of A" THEN "USA"
          ELSE Location
  END AS country,
  access."type" AS access_level,
  --type --replaced by access_level
  CASE
          WHEN Info = "%active" THEN True
          WHEN Info = "%inactive" THEN False
  END AS is_active
FROM
  app.Users
JOIN
  app.access
ON
  Users.type = access.id
WHERE
  is_deleted != True
```

Put It All Together

Figure 10.6 indicates all the types of cleaning we have done.

1. Removed the unused column External_ID by not putting it in our select statement.

2. JOINed in an email field to have a consistent, unique way to reference users.

3. Standardized the encoding for the location field to a consistent country abbreviation and renamed to country.

4. Made *Type* column name easier to understand by renaming it *access_level* and made the values descriptive for what access level lets them do.

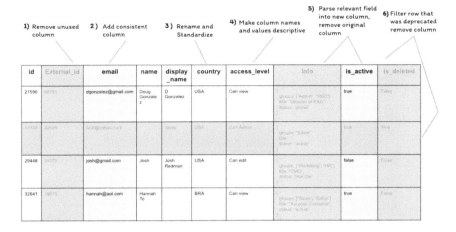

Figure 10.6 indicates all the types of cleaning we have done.

5. Pulled out the status field from the JSON into a new column called is_active and labeled the data true or false accordingly.

6. Used the is_deleted field to filter out deprecated data and then did not include the is_deleted field in the select statement.

In addition, when we renamed each column we put them into snake case. All this work results in what is shown in Figure 10.7. While not all of the data is perfect, it is much more understandable by any business user who would like to query it.

We can combine all of the work we have done and apply it to the remaining fields in a singular query to create the view:

id	email	name	display_name	country	access_level	is_active
21590	dgonzalez@gmail.com	Doug Gonzalez	D Gonzalez	USA	Can view	true
29448	josh@gmail.com	Josh	Josh Redman	USA	Can edit	false
32641	hannah@aol.com	Hannah To		USA	Can view	true

Figure 10.7

```
CREATE VIEW stg_users AS
SELECT
  Id as id,
  -- External_Id -- unused
  Name as name,
  Display Name as display_name,
  contacts.Email as email,
  CASE
            WHEN Location = "United States" THEN "USA"
            WHEN Location = "US" THEN "USA"
            WHEN Location = "US of A" THEN "USA"
            ELSE Location
  END AS country,
  access."type" AS access_level,
  --type --replaced by access_level
  CASE
            WHEN Info = "%active" THEN True
            WHEN Info = "%inactive" THEN False
  END AS is_active
FROM
  app.users
JOIN
app.contacts
  ON users.Id = contacts.Id
JOIN
  app.access
  ON Users.type = access.id
WHERE
  is_deleted != True
```

Now this is starting to look quite complex and hard to maintain. As further transformations are applied, the query will become increasingly large and benefit from having discrete chunks of logic spread across multiple files or changing multiple CTEs that end a final CREATE VIEW query at the bottom.

Other Staging Modeling Considerations

NULLs

There are several "kinds" of NULL values. You may see strings like "N/A" or "null" or true NULL values (remember, a NULL is an absence of a value). What these values stand for can be anything from a missing value, an unknown result, an error, and so on. Your team decides and manages what a NULL value (or one of its look-alikes) indicates.

Because so much business logic can hinge on the meaning of a NULL value in a field, we recommended refraining from replacing NULL fields anytime there's a need to distinguish between an unknown value versus a blank value, or the absence of a value. In today's SQL workbenches, it's very obvious that a field is NULL, whereas an empty string may appear to be the same as a field of whitespace. To a human, there's not too much difference between a true NULL and a string like "null." Warehouses, on the other hand, will treat these very differently for purposes of aggregation and implicit type inference. There are, however, exceptions to this guideline. The right course of action is to assess what your business needs are and understand the caveats involved with forgoing a true NULL value.

Ways of Replacing Nulls
String Values

As mentioned, frequent string replacements for NULLs are "N/A," "Unknown," or "". Using human-readable values can make interpreting data easier, especially when grouping by this type of field. Otherwise, it may not be apparent if the null is a mistake or if it is intentional. However, this is usually done in report models or other "downstream" tables. Sometimes, transformations like this are done in business intelligence tools.

Do note that by replacing a NULL in a field you will impact aggregations such as COUNT. If you do a count DISTINCT on a column that had Stated in it, you will get 51 instead of 50 if there are any missing values.

Numbers

Numbers are trickier to replace since they directly affect aggregated statistics, and NULLs are typically interpreted correctly by SQL aggregations. Sometimes, it is appropriate to replace with 0 when going to visualize data, especially for a line chart over time.

TABLE 10.1   Friends

Name	State	Age
Matt	CA	28
Dave	CA	32
Joy	NULL	30
Lisa	CA	NULL

When the goal is to show there were no sales on a particular day, a 0 will have a value on the chart, whereas a NULL may not display that segment of the line.

This type of replacement is useful but may only get modeled in at the BI tool when doing an individual query.

Dates

At times, NULL date values are represented by "1900-01-01" as an arbitrary date to eliminate NULLs. Using this type of substitution assumes that you do not have any data points with dates existing that far back, but you would need to keep this in mind when querying your date fields as it can cause skewed results.

When Not to Replace

Whenever using aggregation such as MIN(), AVG(), MAX(), SUM(), or COUNT(), NULL values are omitted. For example, COUNT(*) counts all rows, even if one column contains NULL values, whereas COUNT(column_name) omits NULL values from the result. Aggregations with GROUP BY, also group NULL values, in addition to all other values.

Consider Table 10.1 containing NULL values and how aggregation behaves given different cases.

Case 1: NULL integer *Age*

```
SELECT
  AVG(age)
FROM
  friends
```

Result:

AVG(Age)
30

Reason:

(28 + 32 + 30) / 3

Case 2: NULL integer *Age* and NULL CHAR *State*
```
SELECT
  state,
  AVG(age)
FROM
  friends
GROUP by
  state
```

Result:

State	AVG(Age)
CA	30
NULL	30

Reason:

```
CA State group ages = (28+32) / 2 (rows)
NULL State group ages = 30 / 1 (rows)
```

Case 3: COUNT of Friends
```
SELECT
  COUNT(*)
FROM
  friends
```

Result:

COUNT(*)
4

Reason:
```
All rows are considered by COUNT(*)
```

Date and Time

Standardizing time columns is critical to empowering self-serve data use. As teams spread across time zones and transitions, having more remote employees, using Coordinated Universal Time (UTC) format makes date and time data more flexible for them. While using UTC may be confusing to query at first since most people do not live within this time zone, it keeps the company consistent at the database level.

 UTC

Coordinated Universal Time (UTC) is a standard that is time zone agnostic; it is also sometimes referred to as Greenwich Mean Time (GMT). UTC defines the precise time relative to mean solar time at 0° longitude without any adjustments concerning Daylight Saving time. You can convert one time zone to another by subtracting hours based on what time zone you are in. For instance, Pacific Standard Time is 8 hours behind UTC, so if it is 11am in UTC, it is 3am in PST.

Storing time data as UTC means that all records are encoded with a standard time zone, so everyone uses the same time value. Then on top of the database in your BI tool you can update how it interprets the date/time data to fit your analysis. Those values can be localized to whatever local time zone is necessary for a query or report.

Recommended practices:

- Convert all non-UTC date and time columns to UTC.
- Update BI tools to query based on the business's preferred time zone.
- Use a function like CONVERT_TIMEZONE to localize date and time values to a relative time zone.

TABLE 10.2

id	full_name	last_name
21590	Doug Smith	Smith
13107	Josh Fowler	Fowler

TABLE 10.3

Top of SQL comment	Inline comment
```-- dropped unnecessary` ` column last_name` `SELECT` ` id,` ` full_name` `FROM` ` app.users```	```SELECT` ` id,` ` full_name` ` -- last_name dropped` ` unnecessary column` `FROM` ` app.users```

SQL Comments

SQL comments explain specific decisions about why something was coded the way it was. It is best to leave these comments inline so that their context is easily assessed.

For example, let's remove the "last name" column in Table 10.2 because it does not seem necessary for analysis.

```
SELECT
  id,
  full_name
FROM
  dl_table
```

Without a comment it can be difficult to understand why the view was created the way that it was. Some companies adopt a practice of including all columns in the view and commenting them out (Table 10.3).

While this makes it easier to add back in, it may also make it easier to do that unintentionally.

 Trailing/Leading Commas

There is also fierce debate about whether modelers should use leading or trailing commas (Table 10.4). This is because most people write SQL code with trailing commas, but there is a small advantage to leading commas when commenting out columns.

If we comment out the single line in each, there will be an error in the Trailing comma code because we did not go back and remove the comma after "name." Proponents of the trailing comma style argue that it's superior for being able to easily comment out the first column. This is a fierce culture war with no end in sight. Take the strategy that works for your team.

TABLE 10.4

Trailing comma	Leading comma
SELECT id, full_name, -- last_name FROM app.users	SELECT id , full_name -- , last_name FROM app.users

Run the Model

Now, with all these transformation techniques in our toolbelt, let's talk about what it means to build, or "run," a data model. Individual queries are run and the results are fed into a SQL workbench program or perhaps exported to a CSV. Nowadays, SQL interfaces save queries in a notepad-like interface for later. But as you scale a warehouse, you encounter a need to repeat transformation code, as some processing steps are common to what many analyses need.

Suffice to say, this is very inefficient and highly prone not only to logic errors but also lost code. There are a couple of ways today's analysts avoid this problem. First, rather than copying the actual code into queries, we create views directly into our warehouse (as opposed to tables, which will require scheduled rebuilds to load new rows into the data lake). We can choose to materialize them for performance reasons, which we will touch on later in this section.

To tell the original version and "cleaned" version of a data model apart, we recommend creating this view within a new schema where staging models will live. If nothing else, table names will remain identical or at least similar. Aim to be explicit. A little overhead is a worthy trade for a more sensible warehouse layout.

So let's set up a new schema specifically for staging models.

Let's call the new schema "trials." **WARNING:** Be sure this is a new schema name; otherwise, you may delete existing data. We specifically chose "trials" for this in-book example, as this is not a standard term in the industry.

We drop the old version of the schema if it already exists:

```
DROP SCHEMA IF EXISTS trials CASCADE;
```

One workflow for updating staging schemas in the future involves dropping the already existing views (or tables) and "rebuilding the schema and models" using the instructions to follow. This deletion step is required. SQL does not allow in-place UPDATES to the definitions of views (or tables).

Now that we're sure there is no trials schema on disk, we create the schema:

```
CREATE SCHEMA trials;
```

We then set the access to this schema, so that the right user groups can read from these tables (but not write or delete usually):

```
AUTHORIZATION company;
GRANT ALL ON SCHEMA mymodels TO company;
GRANT ALL ON SCHEMA mymodels TO public;
```

Usually, tables are referenced in FROM statements using the format of schema_name.table_name. If a table name is missing a schema name prefix, SQL engines automatically prefix the table name with the schema name "public." Sometimes, warehouse leads find it convenient to set their warehouse's default schema name to something other than "public":

```
SET search_path TO trials;
```

Now, the warehouse engine will assume that all table name references without a schema name reference live in "trials." Databases today can even support multiple schemas in the default search path:

```
SET search_path TO trials, public;
```

After running this command, a warehouse engine will check the trials and public schemas (in this order) for tables that are named without a "schema_name." prefix.

Okay, now that our trial schema exists, we can add tables (again remember, tables here can mean tables *and* materialized views). Altogether the code might look something like what is shown in Figure 10.8.

Running these instructions into a SQL workbench or in a script through an API (e.g. via a SQL library called in a Python script) will create a materialized view that you, and anyone with access, can SELECT from in future queries or materialized views.

Building on Top of Staging Schemas

After we produce a clean version of various source tables of our data, we will then look to combine them in different ways to make it easier for end users to query.

```
                    funnel.sql
    DROP SCHEMA IF EXISTS trials CASCADE;

    CREATE SCHEMA trials
      AUTHORIZATION chartio;
    GRANT ALL ON SCHEMA mymodels TO chartio;
    GRANT ALL ON SCHEMA mymodels TO public;
    SET search_path TO trials, public;

    CREATE VIEW orgs AS
    SELECT * FROM organizations_organizations;

    CREATE MATERIALIZED VIEW actions AS
    SELECT
      oa.organization_id,
      oa.user_id,
      oa.action_activity,
      oa.action_category,
      oa.action_description,
      oa.action_type,
      oa.created_at,
      oa.updated_at,
      oa.user_email,
      o.name,
      o.trial_start_date,
      o.trial_end_date,
      o.started_paying_at is not null AS won,
      (oa.created_at::DATE - o.trial_start_date::DATE + 1) AS day_of_trial,
    FROM organizations_organizationaction oa
    JOIN organizations_organization o ON o.id = oa.organization_id
    WHERE
    (o.trial_start_date > '2014-01-01'
    )]
```

Figure 10.8

For example let's say our hypothetical goal is to build a query that combines a couple of Salesforce tables that we have already cleaned into staging views into a single staging view. A possible use case might be deriving the right strategy for contacting someone based on personal information and their role within a client company.

This is a fairly common straightforward ask, and this relationship may be asked for later on. Hence, we rule it's worth it to construct a table that contains their contact and basic demographic information. This effort saves the end-user time in querying the data warehouse.

That query might look like what is shown in Figure 10.9.

We are choosing a subset of the total possible columns and rolling up/denormalizing the table a bit to make it easier for others to query. As we continue to combine data and make it more usable,

Figure 10.9 A typical SQL query joining tables de-normalized to a new structure.

we are building the data warehouse; the staging steps allow us to build from the bottom up.

Assembling an arsenal of materialized views is a fantastic improvement over ad-hoc SQL files that exist on a shared company directory (or worse, copy-and-paste SQL coding). However, this strategy too has its limits. Increasingly complicated views tend to pull from many tables. Not only that, it's difficult to keep track which version of a materialized view currently lives in your database.

For example, say you and your team decided it'd be better to restructure a query. You spent a fair amount of time updating the SQL query that built the view in the first place. After it's finished, you delete the previous version of the model and build this new one. But, there's a problem: the new version has a bug in it. Did anyone on your team save the old version? You scramble to see if there's any place that a previous version of the code was saved. As you do this, your headache grows worse and worse.

Imagine these types of problems on a multi-person team. For collaborative analytics and a data warehouse to really blossom, your team should employ a tool that stores this code in files and version controls it. While we're cooking up a wish list, imagine what it'd be like to template reusable code and to support your database with a testing framework. There's a lot of features we could ask for.

Luckily for us, dbt (Fishtown analytics' "data build tool") was invented to solve these very problems.

Chapter Eleven

Model Data with dbt

dbt is a lightweight but powerful open source tool built around your SQL files. Consult their online docs on how to install and get started with it. Don't worry, we're not selling you anything—the tool is free and open source.

Now, consider that you *could* build staging schemas without a modeling tool, but it would not be efficient for all the reasons we described earlier. dbt wraps SQL with bookkeeping and a templating language called Jinja precisely to enable teams to write all the transformations they could dream up and manage them at scale.

We'll dive into some of the central features packaged in dbt.

Version Control

Modeling data is an ongoing process. We need a way to update how the modeling code is working and make it easy to see how it was done in the past. Even better would be the ability to revert changes in case a bug is introduced. Version control provides just this.

While version control is ubiquitous in software engineering, this is still a new concept for the analytics world. We will not provide an in-depth tutorial here but would recommend checking out the following resources:

Emilie Schario's post—There is no such thing as a nontechnical data analyst

Udacity's free course—Version Control with Git

Modularity and Reusability

dbt enables organizations to easily define their data in schemas. If something about business logic changes, dbt files can be updated, and, after their changes, will propagate to models and users downstream. This makes it significantly easier for everyone to use the same (hopefully, correct) data. Ensuring everyone has access to the same data is a must for any collaborative analytics team.

Package Management

Software developers often want to reuse code. So should analysts. After all, most companies use a similar set of SaaS tools, so other developers have created useful packages that we can use for free. Some packages help turn page views into sessions, some make working with specific tools in your data stack more manageable, and others have unique functions that might be what we need. dbt has an amazing community. Whenever there is a data challenge that can be solved with some code, check there first to see if a package already exists.

Organizing Files

To model data with dbt, we need a series of SQL-type files (hereafter, .sql) that create our views. dbt keeps things organized with YAML-type (hereafter, .yml) files.

 YAML

YAML stands for "YAML Ain't Markup Language." YAML file extensions are either .yml or .yaml. These files are often used for configuring an application: setting values for names, versions, and ways for files to interact with each other.

Now configuration with code might sound scary, but it is actually quite easy to read and use. Plus dbt autogenerates a starting template for us (Figure 11.1).

Macros

When we have complex case statements, they can be difficult to maintain and hard to read. dbt lets us use the templating language Jinja to write macros. These functions wrap SQL in conditional for-loops and other control-flow logic.

 Jinja

Jinja is a pythonic templating language, so it works how you would expect coding something in python to work. Jinja lets you set local and global variables, work with more complex data types like arrays and dictionaries, build loops, and much more. dbt uses it to generate SQL and documentation for a dbt project.

Note that Jinja can only craft SQL. In other words, it helps with conditional code generation.

Figure 11.1
Source: GitHub, Inc.

For example, the Case statement, which matches location to a country, could be written as a macro in Jinja. This will then be called with one line of code, namely {{ locations() }}.

``
CASE
WHEN Location = "US"
  THEN "USA"
WHEN Location = "UNITED STATES"
  THEN "USA"
WHEN Location = "US of A"
  THEN "USA"
ELSE Location
END AS "Location",
``
	``
	{% macro locations() %}
	
	{% set locations = ['US', 'United States', 'US of A'] %}
	CASE
	{% for location in locations -%}
	  WHEN Location = '{{ location }}' THEN "USA"
	  {% if loop.last %}ELSE Location {% endif -%}
	{% endfor %}
	END
	
	{% endmacro %}
	``

Incremental Tables

To assist with performance, we mostly materialize datasets as views. But this strategy suffers when dealing with very large tables. Materializing an entire table every time an update is needed takes much too long. To alleviate wait-times, dbt supports incremental models, which add new rows to materialized tables instead of recreating the whole model each time the model is rerun.

Testing

In data, garbage in means garbage out. dbt provides out-of-the-box testing to ensure data is meeting a set criteria. We can test both our sources and models that we have built. Common tests check for uniqueness, nulls, accepted values, and if the field exists in another table. However, dbt allows you to build your own custom tests as well as bring in pre-built tests from their hub of packages at hub.getdbt.com.

Lets cover each of the baseline tests to start implementing on sources and staging schemas (Figure 11.2).

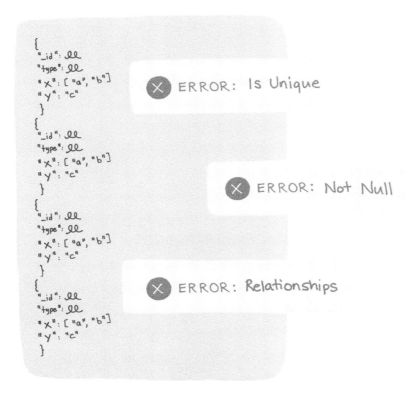

Figure 11.2 Common modeling errors people make.

Uniqueness

For id fields, emails, and other fields that should be unique set up a test by writing a uniqueness test in dbt. This test checks that all the values in the specified column do not have any duplicates. All dbt tests go in the *.yml files that define the sources and models of your dbt project. More information may be found in dbt's Testing documentation.

```
models:
  - name: users
  columns:
   - name: id
   tests:
    - unique
```

Not Null

For id fields, date fields, Booleans, and key fields within a table write a test to ensure the columns have no null values. If there are non-null values found in the column, then the test will not pass.

```
models:
  - name: users
  columns:
   - name: id
   tests:
    - unique
    - not_null
```

A good rule of thumb is that all primary key columns have the uniqueness and not null tests to ensure the proper grain and granularity.

Relationships

To test the relationship of column values between tables, add a relationship test. According to the dbt docs (which we highly recommend reading after this book), relationship tests ensure "that all of the records in a child table have a corresponding record in a parent table."

For example, the following checks that every value of the "user_id" column in the User Teams table has a corresponding value in the parent Users table. The test will not pass if there is a user_id in User Teams that doesn't exist in the Users table.

```
models:
 - name: user_teams
 columns:
  - name: user_id
  tests:
   - relationships:
   to: ref('users')
   field: id
```

Accepted Values

For columns that are expected to have a set list of values, add an Accepted Values test. The test will not pass if any values appear in the column outside of the supplied list.

```
models:
 - name: users
 columns:
  - name: type
  tests:
   - accepted_values:
     values: ['staff', 'moderator', 'end-user']
```

These four tests are a starting point, but you can expand to your use cases, including creating custom tests, or leverage the dbt-expectations package (Figure 11.3). https://discourse.getdbt.com/t/new-package-dbt-expectations/1771

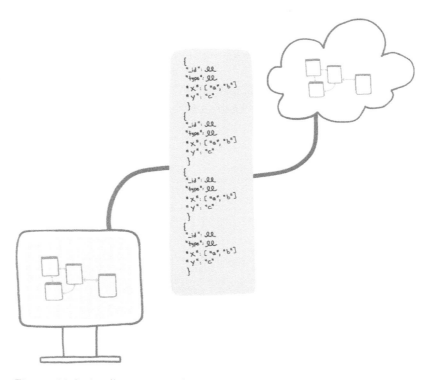

Figure 11.3 An illustration of table entities connected to a local machine synchronized with a cloud service.

Chapter Twelve

Deploy Modeling Code

While building staging schemas begins as the warehouse lead's responsibility, no one is a perfect data modeler. It is best to catch errors and omissions in modeling code as it is being built rather than debugging the entire single source of truth. In this process, we turn to more best practices from the world of software engineering such as comment logic in SQL files and leaving proper commit messages for code reviewers to understand the intent of your changes and implementation details.

Branch Using Version Control Software

There are several version control packages out there for you to choose from. We'll assume you're using Git. As we have said, in collaborative coding environments, it's imperative that you version control your software. A remote backup, hosted, say, through GitHub allows many different people to all contribute to a code base at once.

Using Git, you can create a new development branch to ensure there is always a degree of separation between the main branch of your warehouse transformations and the feature branch you are currently developing on (all of these practices are written about in blogs just a web search away).

When embarking on a new set of transformations, always create a new branch using Git branch -m.

Commit Message

Eventually, someone will work on or around code that someone else has written. When batches of changes to a shared coding project are committed, or saved, to the project, they are labeled with a commit message. These are short messages that communicate at a high level what changes were made and why. As an example:

Git commit -m "Removed External Id column to make table easier for business users"

Giving the reasoning helps people who are reviewing your code assess whether or not your code changes achieved your goal.

Test Locally

As a best practice and basic engineering principle, always test development changes without pushing changes to production. Create a local development environment within a dbt project that creates models in a schema separate from the one used for reports and analyses. Changes can be tested by running dbt locally and querying it from an IDE to explore the data before creating a pull request to submit code changes. This process captures mistakes from typos to dbt tests that didn't pass due to a bad join.

dbt thankfully makes it easy to manage separate development and production environments.

Code Review

Get modeling code reviewed before merging it. This is standard practice in software engineering and is being widely adopted in data teams. This means that before your modeling code is going to reflect on the actual database that you and the rest of your company are using, someone else will verify what you have done, leave comments if they have questions, and approve (or reject) changes based on their understanding of how it works.

Code reviews take place in pull requests. We encourage you to consult any of the great tutorials on how to accomplish this already out there. See GitHub's own guide on the subject.

This fits into a larger agile workflow as visualized in Figure 12.1.

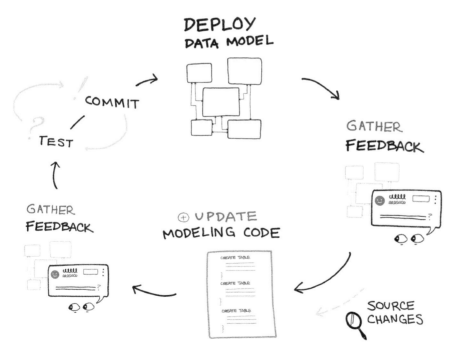

Figure 12.1 Diagram showing the process lifecycle of model updates.

Schedule Runs

Once the code is approved, the model still needs to be run before the new schema will actually be created. We can coordinate with engineering if they have systems for running data models, or if your dbt project is set up on dbt Cloud. There, we can create a job and schedule it to run using cron syntax (Figure 12.2).

Figure 12.2

Chapter Thirteen

Implementing the Data Warehouse

Remember, staging schemas hold transformations that build on top of the data sources residing in a data lake. In general, different sources track the same events or users in different ways and places. To get the most use of our company data, it's useful to combine these different sources into new tables that make future analyses simple and straightforward to write. After all, there's no need for a team to reference multiple staging tables containing user information in dozens of queries or models when an intermediate staging model could be built on top of the basic transformations we've so far completed to unite the user data.

This is an iterative process of trying out different ways to combine data to make it more useful for end users. The intermediate transformations needed to build combined tables fill up a warehouse fast. Before diving into the individual tables, we want to first touch on a key tool that should guide and inform your warehouse design.

Manage Dependencies

When staging models, select from their source replicas; we say that the staging models "depend" on their respective source replicas. This is the language of mathematical graphs. Using the language of graph theory proves an extremely useful tool when trying to keep track of dozens, if not hundreds, of data models in a mature warehouse. In particular, a large interconnected network of models can be visualized as a Directed Acyclic Graph (Figure 13.1).

Let's introduce some basic dependency language first. Imagine if node a in Figure 13.1 were a source replica and nodes b through e were different kinds of transformations. Nodes b through e are said to be "downstream" from node a. So, all transformations are downstream from the source replica represented by node a. Likewise, node a is "upstream" of all other models. Models can be more or less "upstream" or "downstream" from one another. The power of this tool and language lies in its ability to visualize the relationship between entities that comprise a warehouse.

Figure 13.1

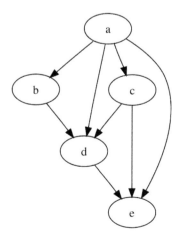

Directed Acyclic Graph

A directed acyclic graph or DAG is a connection of items that only flows in one direction. This lets us be sure that the transformations we are applying to data are not self-referential and create a loop.

Our transformational tool of choice, dbt, has a built-in method of building a dependency graph of your data warehouse's transformations. Run the *dbt docs generate* and *dbt docs serve* commands in the repo, which houses your modeling code. Barring any errors in transformations code, these produce a DAG (Figure 13.2).

We can see the staging views that we built on top of our original sources. In Figure 13.2, sources belong to two different schemas. We add a staging model for cleaning purposes because we intend to use each of these tables in our warehouse in some way. By cleaning, the data can then be transformed and combined together to build our data warehouse. After some basic cleaning and source mixing, you may end up with an iteration of the DAG (Figure 13.3).

In Figure 13.3, we alter the names of different transformations to make better logical sense of what's happening technically. This scheme of transformation is just one way it may make sense to design your model flow. For example, the salesforce.users source may not be fully staged until accessing a field from salesforce.user_roles.

 Figure 13.2

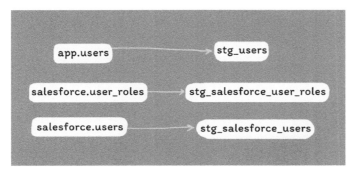

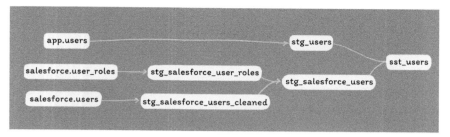

Figure 13.3

Hence, we clean the users table as much as possible, then build a completely prepared model for this source prefixed stg_.

After doing staging work, users can access the combined and enriched tables at the end of your DAG for analysis. The end tables are our single source of truth; they are the useful abstractions on top of our source data.

From these examples, we aim to show that dependency graph DAGs reflect the transformations that comprise a database. These organize the many dozens of transformations a robust warehouse over time acquires. It helps anyone visualize the flow of information from sources to completed reports. And in a data literate company, this tool can inform non-subject-matter-experts where to look for the information they are seeking; the more downstream the model, the more likely tables will be accessible and have what they actually want.

Armed with a DAG, a data team can work to secure data, control the grain of information across the organization, and efficiently calculate metrics. Let's talk through some strategies for building layers on top of the staging views.

Combine Tables Within Schemas

Recall that transactional databases are in 3NF because they must minimize repeated data. Repetition is bad, because if, for instance, a country ever changes its name, potentially millions of records need updating. There are plenty of ways to mess up this process or miss rows outright that need updating. In a perfectly normalized schema, the country name should only be listed once in the database and then joined on other tables via a foreign key. This lets us update the name once while keeping the key the same everywhere. Another nice benefit to that is it saves a lot of storage space.

But for Analytics (OLAP) databases, we don't need to optimize tables for space (thanks, C-store compression!), and we don't have to manage updates since we never write to/update analytics tables. Transformations are a chain of SELECTs working together to make data insights available. In other words, we create "repetition friendly" views *on top of* a normalized database. This opposite process is fittingly called denormalizing.

Whereas normalizing data helps the machine, denormalizing helps the analyst. For example, it can be convenient to create a wide table (materialized as a view) that contains pre-joined results. These wide tables can sit alongside the normalized version in the data warehouse. We can create these joins between staging views to create useful views for analysis (Figure 13.4).

Like with any query, be cautious about the type of JOIN used when creating wide tables. JOINs can produce duplicate data or introduce NULLs into tables if done incorrectly. For instance, an INNER JOIN on zendesk.users and application.users might cause some users in the application to disappear from the resulting data because not all application users might have filed a ticket in zendesk yet. If we then INNER JOINed zendesk.tickets to this table, we would have all the

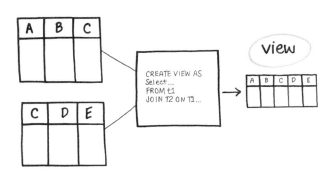

Figure 13.4 A diagram of two tables joined to create a wider table.

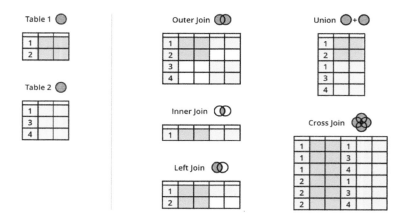

Combining Data Tables – SQL Joins Explained

A JOIN clause in SQL is used to combine rows from two or more tables, based on a related column between them.

Figure 13.5

user information duplicated for each ticket that user created. That would mean a COUNT(*) of the table would no longer give us an accurate count of the number of users in our database.

Examine Figure 13.5 to see which type of join will bring in what rows from each table.

Combine Tables Across Schemas

Take, for example, a company tracks sign-ups via Hubspot, and after a year, decides to switch to Salesforce. The Salesforce table has no record of the sign-ups that occurred in the past that were tracked by Hubspot. When an analyst attempts to query for sign-ups, it is unclear which data source they should use and how they might combine it properly (Figure 13.6).

Companies end up using new tools to track the same type of data. In these instances, migrate the data from the previous tools into the latest tool. If this is not an option, use the data warehouse to create a view that UNIONs the data from both sources (Figure 13.7).

Figure 13.6

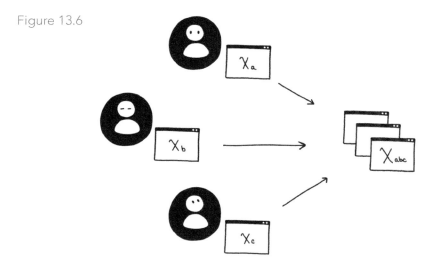

Consolidating data sources ensures the historical records are not lost and creates one location for relevant metrics. Compounding data sources this way requires some renaming and cleaning to accomplish.

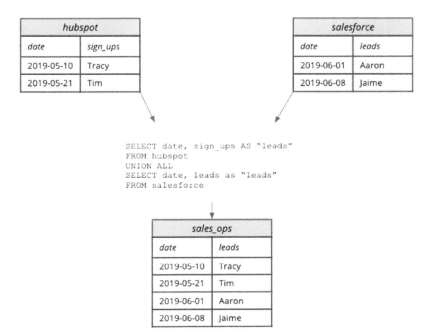

Figure 13.7 Two tables, combined with a UNION SQL statement.

We might want to further generate a new unique key for this union.

Another example with a more complex join would be if we have invoice tables from two different sources; a full outer joined result can make one universal invoice table that is easy to read:

```
SELECT
  o.order_id,
  o.order_quantity,
  o.item_total,
  o.order_total,
  c.customer_id,
  c.first_name,
  c.last_name,
  c.company,
FROM
  customers c
FULL OUTER JOIN
  orders o ON o.customer_id = c.customer_id
```

Keep the Grain Consistent

When creating a table that will be used for analytics, be sure that the grain is intuitive from the table name. For example, consider a table named orders (Table 13.1).

TABLE 13.1   Orders

Order_item_id	order_id	price	quantity
27	15	5	1
28	15	10	1
29	16	6	1
30	17	7	1

But wait, this table describes the items of an order, not the orders themselves. To obtain an orders table, we need to apply some aggregation, such as using a group by clause to obtain the desired result (Table 13.2).

TABLE 13.2

Order_item_id	order_id	price
27	15	15
29	16	6
30	17	7

Always keep in mind downstream users of data and what they expect to see when they aggregate. Make sure that rows have been "rolled up" accordingly. The rows of a table should represent one unit of the entity the table is supposed to represent.

Create Business Metrics

There are a lot of different ways to measure how a business is performing. Some are relatively well known, such as "Monthly Active Users" or "Number of Trials Started." Establishing an accurate metric such as these is difficult because the data for a metric calculation may exist in multiple sources and the business logic behind them can change.

Metrics are also highly sensitive to levels of granularity, and they typically obfuscate some filtering decisions, so it is important to be careful with how they are calculated and documented. We should focus on getting the right grain and creating calculated fields that make it easier to determine aggregated metrics.

Adding Calculated Fields to Tables

Let's say we want an orders table and we want a profit margin per order field, but currently there is a line item for every order item. We first need to roll up the cost and revenue of the order items into one row per order, and then we can calculate the profit per order. Doing this roll-up also allows us to aggregate and produce metrics such as the total number of orders and average cost, revenue, and profit margin per order.

These types of values enrich the data and make it easier for analysts to find more insights within it. Analysts can join this table with other tables and segment and leverage it in many ways.

Avoid Aggregated Metric Tables

Defining metrics in rows is great, but leave the aggregating of those metrics to the BI tool. If you pre-aggregate them, then it removes the ability to slice and dice the metric. Occasionally, it can be beneficial if you have a ton of data and you regularly look at it by some high-level date grouping such as quarter or year where it takes significant computation to produce these metrics. In these instances, materialize the view but remember this prevents more exploration of the data; investigate scaling up your database before reducing how the data can be explored.

Create a Standard Metrics Dashboard

Another tactic for defining aggregated metrics is to create a well-documented dashboard and query. Provide text on the dashboard that explains the calculations needed to produce the metric and leave more specific SQL comments describing the filters being used (Figure 13.8).

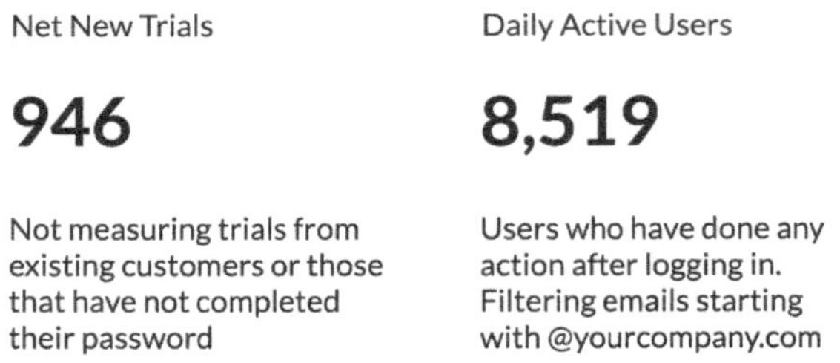

Figure 13.8 A screenshot from a dash showing a metric for new trials and daily active users with metric descriptions.

Net New Trials

946

Not measuring trials from existing customers or those that have not completed their password

Daily Active Users

8,519

Users who have done any action after logging in. Filtering emails starting with @yourcompany.com

While this is not scalable, it is a quick solution to get a team on the same page. It can be especially useful in earlier stages or when the team is experimenting with metrics.

Keeping Accurate History

When rows of data are updated, we lose that information to history. Maybe a customer started on a smaller plan but upgraded to a higher plan, and the plan field in our database likely got overwritten. If all that exists in the database is what their current plan is, we have no way of recognizing that expansion and no way to look back at what the revenue for that customer might have been two years ago.

When someone starts using the product they are active and we might store the data in our database as in Table 13.3.

TABLE 13.3

Id	email	is_active
1	dave@company.com	TRUE

But after a week the user stops using the tool and is now inactive (Table 13.4).

TABLE 13.4

Id	email	is_active
1	dave@company.com	FALSE

If we wanted to know how many active users there were in the past, we would have no way to query for that with this data model. We have overwritten the field; we would need to determine it.

How should we address this problem?

Snapshots

Computing and storage is relatively cheap, so we can actually store snapshots of what the data was at different times in order to query that data correctly. Once again, dbt has our back. You can configure dbt to create timestamped rows when a particular value changes so that you can access the data in whichever state (Table 13.5).

TABLE 13.5

Id	email	is_active	dbt_valid_from	dbt_valid_to
1	dave@company.com	TRUE	1/1/2020	1/14/2020
1	dave@company.com	FALSE	1/14/2020	*NULL*

dbt can be configured to know when to check for new values and which values should signal to add a new row to the snapshots.

Keep a Data Log

Some argue to keep track of every update to the DB timestamped in an append-only fashion. This makes it possible to recreate the state of the warehouse at any given time. You can select whatever part of the database history you want to be given a timestamp (WHERE time time_stamp > {start} AND time_stamp < {end}. For rows where a value changed during this time, you need to consider how that would impact your query-and-build models that transform it to be useful. Thankfully, tools like dbt work with Version control so you can try out different paths to getting the modeling correct for different types of analyses.

Chapter Fourteen

Managing
Data Access

A fundamental benefit of the data warehouse lies in the self-serve ability of data and cross-company access to information. More groups than just the centralized data team commonly have access to data warehouses. The data has been cleaned, standardized, and organized. It is self-documenting. Anyone with a bit of SQL know-how can query tables and extract the information they need. A warehouse improves the data literacy across an organization.

However, companies handle information that you may *not* want easily accessible, especially in health systems or anything similar that manages sensitive information. Many security regulations mandating data access rules now exist, such as GDPR, and many companies have industry-standard compliance rules that they adhere to as well, like SOC and HIPAA. Whether it is personally identifiable information (PII) or financial information, sensitive data is much more prevalent throughout a product's journey and the data warehouse than one might think. It's crucial to ensure adequate restrictions on sensitive information in the data warehouse are in place.

Build data restrictions into your warehouse framework as it is built. Even at the start of building your warehouse, answer a few common-sense questions:

- Where is sensitive data (PII and financial) currently handled?
- Will this sensitive data still be present in the data warehouse and then cleaned up?
- How will this information be removed or restricted from the exposed datasets—scripts on the way to the warehouse, data marts created from the warehouse?

Address these questions before connecting BI tools to the warehouse when sensitive information is involved. In the next section are common strategies for securing data and anonymizing it. We also touch on good rules of thumb for managing data access within BI tools. But note: we recommend that the warehouse do more of the heavy lifting.

It's significantly more straightforward to forgo selecting a field into a staging table or obscuring columns during staging transformations than it is securing dashboards for different teams or individuals. And with a few GRANT commands, individual tables or schema in your database can surface to only certain persons by default. Also, thinking in terms of staging tables and what kinds of transformations in the database can protect sensitive data prepares our infrastructure for organizing transformations with data marts, the upcoming (and last) stage of a modern data stack we cover in this text.

For now, let's explore the warehouse-level methods of securing your warehouse (Figure 14.1).

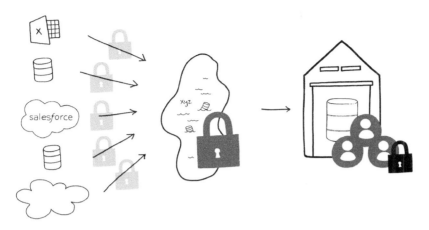

Figure 14.1 The stages of agile data organization showing how security for most users moves to the data warehouse.

How to Secure Sensitive Data in the Data Warehouse

The most direct way to limit access to the proper people is to enforce rules at the warehouse. Create read-only replicas, make custom user groups with different access permissions, and fully encrypt particularly sensitive data.

 Handling Sensitive Data with Managed Solutions

This area of the book mainly pertains to unmanaged warehouse engines such as Redshift that provide much more modularity requiring resource management. For warehouse engines like BigQuery and Snowflake, there's no need to replicate or deal with infrastructure because those solutions automatically scale. Therefore, you only need to copy the tables or apply access restrictions to the data directly.

Read-Only

As we did with a read-only replica for the production database and the data lake, it's best practice to set up a warehouse to be read-only by default. Modern data modeling with tools like dbt is done through transformation layers on top of the data. Rather than thinking in terms of UPDATE and DELETE, think in terms of SELECT.

If nothing else, transformations on source tables should be idempotent. By that, we mean that you should be able to destroy a table outright and reconstruct the warehouse state as it was (assuming no stateful tables like sources or snapshots were irreparably lost). The value of this lies in resilience but also simplicity. Analysts can think in terms of SELECTs and let the code they write manage data for them. Whereas one-off stateful commands are difficult to log, anyone reading transformation code can see exactly what rows are being removed during table construction (and if well-commented, why).

Custom User Groups

Regardless of creating the read-only slave warehouse, create a new user group that has read access only. It's possible to choose to exclude access to specific tables or columns of data from that new user group. Also, it's possible to restrict access to row-specific data. Applying row-level permissions allows the ability to grant full access to tables containing sensitive information but at the same time restricts which rows and values the person querying can see. Depending on the underlying database, configuring row-level permissions differs slightly.

 Row-level Permissions

A great example of when to use row-level permissions is adhering to HIPAA compliance when accessing a hospital's dataset (Figure 14.2). Each doctor within this hospital has access to their

Figure 14.2 Warehouse resources with security protocols applied.

own patients' records for analysis and review. However, we want to prevent every doctor from having access to every patient's medical records. Implementing access controls at the row level by account/patient ownership (whether that is a patient id, patient name) prevents doctors from having the chance to access a patient's personal information they don't need.

You can apply this example to other groups as well: sales teams, customer tracking, and employee records. This gets complicated, and we recommend avoiding it if you can in the warehouse stage. Try using marts in the next section instead to scope down access.

Hash Sensitive Data

When grouping or aggregating sensitive data, creating hashed versions of the data is a reasonable option.

 Hashing

Hashing is the process of inputting any string or number and getting back a consistently long string that is random and called a hash. Incrementing the original number or changing one letter in the string should produce a hash that is completely unrelated to the previous one.

For example:

abc -> hash function -> deioa8f9e

abd -> hash function -> 32131mo

Then users can create summary tables where sensitive metrics, like financial data, can be aggregated to a level that is appropriate for different departments to see and analyze. The level of security implemented will limit what type of analysis can be performed on the data, but does ensure that the sensitive data is protected.

Pseudo-Anonymize Data

One option that mitigates the risk of unintended disclosure involves pseudo-anonymizing PII (personally identifiable information) such as names or addresses, especially when the end consumer of data is a third party. An example would be to remove the names and addresses of patients from a view, so they are unidentifiable by anyone accessing their data in the warehouse.

How to Secure Sensitive Data in a BI Tool

Setting up the right permissions on the database alone does not prevent the inappropriate sharing of sensitive data if you surface sensitive information through a dashboard or report. This type of issue can be challenging to prevent, so the common strategy is to set policies with groups of users in the BI tool. But in truth, sensitive data should be obscured as soon as possible, as we mentioned earlier. We recommend using the strategies already mentioned to ensure models that reports draw from have sensitive data obscured.

Consistent Account Audit/Cleanup

Sometimes the size of the enterprise requires additional auditing. Projects change, roles change, and use cases change. Any of these changes can impact employee permissions. Outdated permissions can lead to compliance and privacy issues. Periodically reviewing and updating permissions is a best practice to protect sensitive data.

During an audit, check all the previous questions we talked about:

- Who has access to which data sources?
- Who has access to sensitive row-level information?
- Who is on the admin team or has admin access?
- Who has access to or is viewing dashboards and reports containing sensitive data?

BI tools offer answers to these questions through varying levels of usage information in-app for the admins to monitor and review. If not all the pieces of information needed are available, talk to the support team of the BI tool. They can help pull the necessary information to make informed decisions about an account's security. Feel free to push the boundaries, because it's amazing what information is available when asked. It's important to make sure data access is controlled and current to today's needs.

Chapter Fifteen

Maintaining the Source of Truth

Now that the data warehouse is set up with an established warehouse lead, the next and ongoing step is maintenance. This involves making sure the data warehouse objects, columns, tables, views, and schemas are accurate and up-to-date. Maintaining a data warehouse is integral for users in an organization to easily and accurately gain insights into data. If it is not maintained, people will query the wrong data and get conflicting results.

As a company's data warehouse ages:

- New metrics need to be tracked.
- Some old metrics are no longer needed.
- Permissions will need to be granted, updated, and revoked (more than expected).

- Modeling will become un-optimized.
- More people will be modeling.

These inevitable problems make it difficult for a company to conduct analyses. To prevent these issues, a data engineer familiar with the data warehouse becomes necessary to know how users are querying the source. This section will go in-depth on these issues and how to address them with routine maintenance (Figure 15.1).

Figure 15.1

Track New Metrics

The ways that businesses measure their success change over time. New products launch, users behave differently, and new predictive models need to factor in new data. Success of the business depends on its ability to react to change. Sometimes this means creating a new calculated field or a new column, view, or table which can then be aggregated into a metric.

We may add a new field to track our customer information in Salesforce that is in line with our new company objectives, say, tracking account activities through the services we provide. From here, we can see what services are most popular with our customers, then offer special promotions on these services during seasonal trends where we see a fall in purchases to increase sales.

Three Considerations for Adding New Calculated Fields

When engineers or analysts create new tables, columns, or views to track data, they do not always follow the naming conventions that fit the data warehouse. This makes interpretation challenging for an analyst unfamiliar with the new metrics.

This unfamiliarity can also create duplicate work—for instance, when creating a view for a support team lacks pertinent information that doesn't distinguish the purpose of the view. Users looking to query this view may not know it exists. In this case, other users are also likely to create a new version of the same view expressing the same information.

1. Where It Should Live

A new calculated field could have a number of different places it could live, and deciding on the best spot can be an art. Do we only need to add the data to an existing table or should we add to a view or create a whole new view? Let's review what reasons we would do each:

Existing Table

- The new calculated field can be understood and queried easily without complex joins or being aggregated.

Existing View*

- A view that exists that is relevant to the new calculated field.
- That view is aggregated in a way that fits this data and its dependent calculated fields.

- Complex join paths would make it difficult for people to query the new data accurately without the view.

New View*

- No view that exists that is relevant to the new calculated field.
- No view that is relevant is aggregated in a way that fits how this calculated field should be aggregated without the view.
- Complex join paths would make it difficult for people to query the new calculated field accurately.

*Typically, it will be added to an existing table as well, but it will be queried from the View.

2. How to Backfill It

It is advisable to backfill data whenever we can determine what the values should be (Figure 15.2). In a categorical column, we might be able to determine the value based on other columns or an obvious default value to enter. If we are not able to determine or have no obvious default value, leave the value as null. However, do consider the impact of NULLs, such as in aggregation. If this impacts the query, try determining a stand-in value such as "Unknown" to indicate it wasn't possible to backfill.

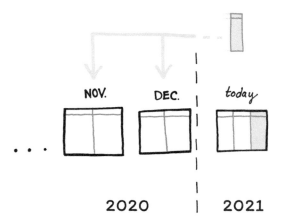

Figure 15.2 Data being backfilled.

In a numeric field the impact of NULLs can be more significant. The other negative of NULLs in a table with time-based data is that it limits analysis to when the new column was added. Sometimes this issue can be overcome by bringing in data from previous data sources or by inputting values based on overall statistics or dimensions of each row.

3. What to Call It

Often data modelers forget to follow their own data warehouse naming conventions when adding new calculated field or updating existing ones. This defeats the point of the warehouse, which needs data to be consistent so others can easily interpret it. Always check your style guide before creating a new column.

Deprecate Old Metrics

As companies grow, the tools they use to spin off data change. Multiple tools might contain similar if not the same types of data, such as having both Hubspot and Salesforce. Which should an analyst use? We want to prevent inaccurate data from being queried so others do not reach inaccurate conclusions.

Even if data sources stay constant, business objectives may change. This can affect what data is appropriate for analysis as well. Features or products might become deprecated as a result, and therefore their associated metrics might be misleading if the analysts are not aware of this.

Explicitly Deprecate Data

While removing difficult-to-use tables and columns prevents people from using them wrongly, sometimes it is not practical to remove them. In this case, we recommend pre-pending the names for these objects to "deprecated_" or "do_not_use_." This naming convention makes it clear to everyone if they are useful when browsing or querying (Figure 15.3).

The style rule of pre-pending "deprecated_" to fields is the best way to manage analysts aggregating it for metrics because it's apparent to everyone that the data should not be used. It's also worth letting users know that these fields and metrics are no longer useful through email or with any BI tools, to avoid catching anyone off guard. Again, naming conventions play an integral role in keeping users from querying data warehouse objects incorrectly.

Many BI tools also provide a query log to help identify what dashboards and charts are using which fields. This makes it easy to let others know if they need to update their queries or deprecate their charts and dashboards.

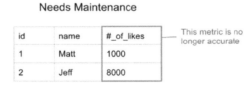

Needs Maintenance

id	name	#_of_likes
1	Matt	1000
2	Jeff	8000

This metric is no longer accurate

Deprecation Options

Naming Convention

id	name	deprecated_#_of_likes
1	Matt	1000
2	Jeff	8000

Drop column /
Create view without that column

id	name
1	Matt
2	Jeff

Figure 15.3 A table with a deprecated metric and two strategies for renaming it.

Staging Schemas Make Source Changes Easy

While we are relying on out-of-the-box tools such as Fivetran to consistently pull in data from our various data sources, there are still times when the data sources change what they are providing. With a staging schema, it makes accommodating this simple. We can update small portions of the query for the view without affecting downstream views that rely on it.

For example, someone may have changed a field name in Salesforce from SL to Sales Qualified Lead. I can update my staging view from this:

```
SELECT
        SL AS sales_qualified_lead
FROM
        salesforce.user
```

To the new column name coming in from salesforce:

```
SELECT
        "Sales Qualified Lead" AS sales_qualified_lead
FROM
        Salesforce.user
```

Since my field was already aliased, all of my downstream tables built on top will not break and do not need to be updated.

Deprecate Old Schemas

Now that we have layered on views and created a new schema for our SST, should we discourage using source schemas and interim staging schemas in our BI tool? Yes. However, it can be helpful to maintain the ability to access old and unused data sources from a data lake in a data warehouse when debugging or finding new modeling opportunities. Label the data sources as "deprecated" or "approved" to make it clear to users in the BI tool which data they should use for their analysis (Figure 15.4).

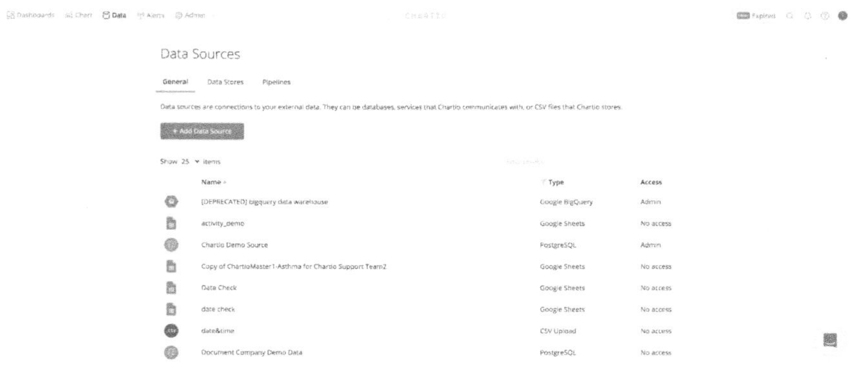

Figure 15.4
Source: Chartio

Resolve Conflicting Numbers

Sometimes metrics show different numbers even though they measure the same thing (Figure 15.5). For example, when the number of new trials in HubSpot is different from the production database, the rule of thumb is to trust the data source closest to the event that tracks it. In this case, it would be the production database:

```
SELECT
  SUM(arr)
FROM
  app.users
WHERE
  trial_start > NOW()::date - 7
  AND email != "%chartio.com"
```

Vs.

```
SELECT
  SUM(arr)
FROM
  app.users
WHERE
  trial_start > NOW()::date - 7
```

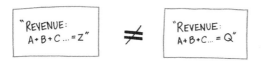

Figure 15.5

Oftentimes, people's calculation of a metric will differ because of the following reasons: they are calculating it based on a different formula; the data source they are using is different; the data is being filtered differently; or there is an error in their calculation.

Track down what the correct answer is and modify the models to be clearer, so both parties and others will calculate the aggregate metric accurately.

Handling Ongoing Requests and Ongoing Feedback

Now your newly modeled data will be queried by various analysts and employees. Inevitably the modeling demands will shift and evolve. Examples of feedback you may get on the models are requests to add new tables or columns, redefine business logic, fix broken tables due to a change in the source system, or investigate incorrect numbers.

For instance, with these new tables someone may want to use the external id from that original table for an analysis. They will not be able to query it from the view. How should they let you know that they are constrained by the current data model?

We recommend using a ticketing system like JIRA (Figure 15.6), GitHub issues, or Google Forms for your users to submit to the analytics engineering team to request changes or additions to the data models.

Figure 15.6 Screenshot of a Chartio Jira project board.
Source: Chartio

This way requests can be tracked, the analytics engineers know what tasks they need to do next, and users can easily see the status of each request. In order for users outside the core team to also help edit the modeling code, they will need to copy the repository locally and know how to use Git.

To read more on intake forms for data requests check out: https://caitlinhudon.com/2020/09/16/data-intake-form/.

Updating Modeling Code

Do not build a new view to fix the modeling code. Rewrite the original modeling code, which will make it easier to maintain and also is consistent with evolving the data model.

So we can rewrite the code to include that column again:

```
SELECT
  Id as id,
  external_id as org_id,
  Name as name,
  Display Name as display_name,
  contacts.Email as email,
  CASE
            WHEN Location = "United States" THEN "USA"
            WHEN Location = "US" THEN "USA"
            WHEN Location = "US of A" THEN "USA"
            ELSE Location
  END AS country,
  CASE
            WHEN Type = "1" THEN "Can view"
            WHEN Type = "2" THEN "Can edit"
            WHEN Type = "3" THEN "Can admin"
  END AS access_level,
  CASE
            WHEN Info = "%active" THEN True
            WHEN Info = "%inactive" THEN False
  END AS is_active
FROM
  app.users
JOIN
  app.contacts
  ON users.Id = contacts.Id
WHERE
  is_deleted != True
```

We can also make sure the commit message explains why this id was added back in: -m "Changed the name of external_id to Org_ id to make table easier for business users."

Manage Access

Not being able to access the required data halts analysis. Similarly, not removing someone's access can be a legal liability. This trade-off must be considered carefully so that permissions do not hinder the productive employees analysis and are not improperly exposing data.

Another concern may be costs. Consider a scenario where users are working on BigQuery, which charges per amount of data queried. To prevent users from abusing queries and raising the cost, create a custom quota. As the BigQuery documentation outlines, a custom quota manages costs by specifying a limit on the amount of query data processed per day. Setting a daily quota on the project-level or at the user-level is a flexible option. This type of permission aims to manage cost while providing permissions to manage data integrity. There are even dbt packages, such as the Snowflake Spend, that can help with tracking costs involved with your warehouse.

A final concern is data loss. While some databases such as Oracle offer the ability to recover a dropped table, some data warehouses do not. While some systems like Snowflake enable you to leverage time travel, when dropping a table in PostgreSQL, it's not possible to restore the table unless restoring from a backup. If it's not possible to restore from a backup, there's no way to recover the dropped table. To avoid this, ensure that the proper individuals have the right permissions on the right data warehouse objects. Everyone analyzing the data should have read-only access.

How to Handle Permissions Correctly

Ensuring that BI Tools access levels mirror the employment status of your employees helps track users and prevents security issues. The main priority of granting permission is to prevent users from accessing sensitive information or from permanently deleting data by accident.

We recommend setting user permissions at a team level because as businesses scale and add more users, it's easier to track than creating custom access for every employee. Tracking individuals in a small company is trivial since they know everyone by name—when new people are hired or when they leave. In large companies, the warehouse lead doesn't know the vast majority of the people they work with or when their roles or employment status change.

Sharing accounts is an unfortunate practice that is important to track. Sharing accounts makes it impossible to hold users responsible for what actions they carried out. If there needs to be an answer as to why a user dropped a table or updated a column, multiple people may need questioning to learn why. Data loss can also be a potential breach of an agreement a company has with its customers and their expectations of how their data is handled. We recommend giving each user a separate account. Separate accounts ensure security compliance and accountability in the event of an error.

We recommend programmatically adding and removing users to avoid employees from being blocked and to ensure they do not maintain access to data they should not have (Figure 15.7). When deciding to add, remove, or change user privileges manually, be vigilant in completely removing/updating the permissions.

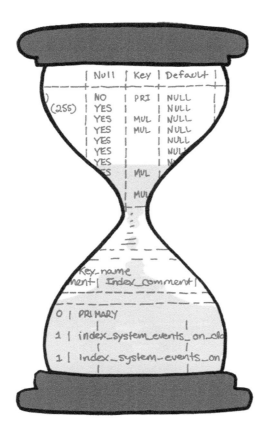

Figure 15.7

Tuning to Optimize

As a company grows, the data that is queried changes, too. New data, new analysts, and new business objectives will shift what data is being queried. The original structure of Data Warehouse objects may need to be reconfigured to optimize usage and performance based on how it is queried.

Different data warehouses will have options to check performance, but most offer ways to:

- Scale up the cluster.
- Materialize expensive views.

Add Clusters

The fastest way to get more performance is to simply add more clusters to the warehouse engine. Many have settings that allow for automatically adding additional clusters if there are many con-current queries taking place. For others, you may need to specify exactly how many clusters to spin up for your instance.

 Clusters

A cluster is the compute resource for a data warehouse engine. It can have several nodes that coordinate the computation needed. Many can be used to perform aggregations for multiple people at the same time.

Materialize Expensive Views

Creating the single source of truth helps users unfamiliar with the structure of the data by consolidating what they need to query to a single place. However, if many tables are being joined to build these helpful views, we may run into some performance issues. There are now a multitude of views within the DAG that people are querying from, so which views might benefit from being materialized? Oftentimes, the final views being materialized can help. In addition, look for places in the DAG where many sources flow into one view. Joins can be expensive on columnar databases, so try materializing those to see if it improves performance.

Code Review All Modeling

Modeling code changes should always be submitted in a pull request and reviewed by a colleague and the Warehouse Lead before being merged to the master branch (Figure 15.8). This will

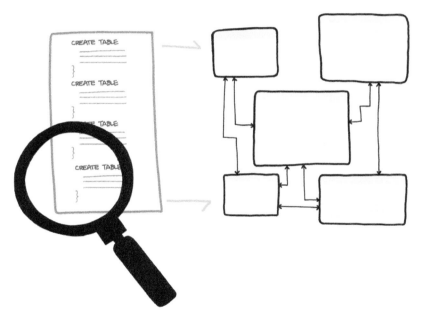

Figure 15.8 Any modeling code should be peer reviewed before it is incorporated into the schema.

ensure that any code has fewer mistakes, follows the proper conventions, and is communicated to the team.

Here is a summary of things to look out for when reviewing a colleague's code changes:

- Is the code following naming and coding conventions?
- Have dbt tests been added as needed?
- Do the proposed changes make the data cleaner or easier to use or accomplish a defined purpose?
- Does the data return expected results?
- Have all model dependencies been considered?
- Are there any typos or syntax errors?

Additionally, dbt has a great article on reviewing analytics pull requests.

Maintenance Checklist

A single source of truth data warehouse is a worthwhile investment. However, without maintenance, it will fall into disarray and lose its value.

- As metrics are added, make sure they're named properly.
- As metrics are deemed no longer useful, make sure they're removed to avoid confusion.
- As metrics need to be updated/pre-aggregated, remember to name them properly.
- Keeping user permissions appropriate and accurate will free up database admins to focus on important projects as well as avoid data being removed accidentally.

- Considering the restructuring of data warehouse objects will help create a suitable structure for analysis and complex querying along with cutting down performance cost.
- The worthwhile investment of a data engineer to perform said maintenance tasks will remove the bottleneck of incorrect analytics from a neglected warehouse.

STAGE 4
DATA MARTS
aka Data Democratized

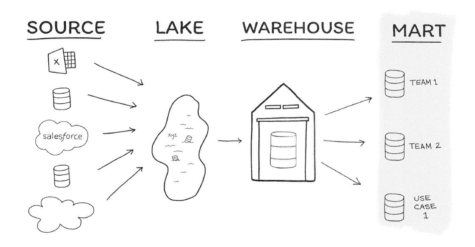

Mart Stage Overview

At long last, we've arrived at the top of the data stack. For these final pages, we consider what makes a data mart. That is, we discuss how to further structure and group data in your warehouse not only to meet one set of needs, but to meet the needs of a number of departments whose business logic may differ from one another.

Stage 4: Data Marts

More data and more schemas will eventually make the data warehouse difficult to navigate. A data mart is a filtered (and sometimes aggregated) subsection of a data warehouse that makes it easier for a particular group to query data. It provides a smaller schema with only the relevant tables for that group.

Overview of Building Data Marts

For warehouses, we needed a warehouse lead to implement the modeling. For data marts, we'll need multiple mart leads. They will determine which tables from the data warehouse are needed for their individual marts (Figure P.1). The mart leads can then customize tables for different use cases. Aggregations, metric calculations, and PII can all be handled individually for teams. However, if there is a metric that needs to be used by multiple teams, the warehouse lead should implement it on the data warehouse.

Figure P.1 Data marts are subsections of a data warehouse schema.

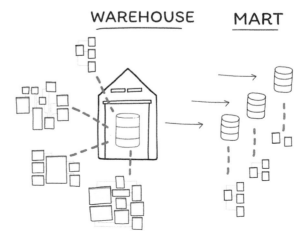

One of the main benefits of setting up a data mart accurately is the ability to scale. There are more people tracking data quality, and data is limited for each team, reducing potential security concerns.

Center Around Business Use Cases

As an organization scales the amount of data it is tracking, the number of people who want to access it scales, too. This results in more people with less context in a large portion of the schema.

We want to go from a large complex schema (Figure P.2) to a series of focused schemas, where each department can quickly find the data they need (Figure P.3).

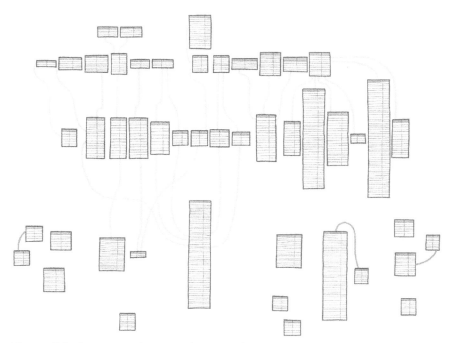

Figure P.2 An entire data warehouse schema.

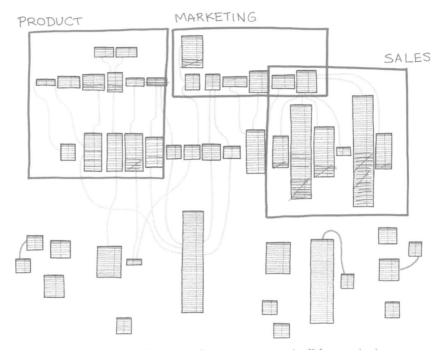

Figure P.3 A data warehouse schema sectioned off for each department's data mart.

Figure P.4 Data warehouse inventory by department needs.

TABLE	PRODUCT	MARKETING	SALES
USER	✓	✗	✓
MARKETING CHANNEL	✗	✓	✓
LEADS	✗	✓	✓

So while going from lake to warehouse was mostly about cleaning up tables, going from warehouse to marts is about centering schemas and tables around business processes and teams. Different departments need different parts of the data warehouse schema (Figure P.4).

Data mart schemas are not very different from data warehouses because the data should already be understandable from the cleaning done in the warehouse stage. Data marts further simplify the schema for people within departments to find what data they need more quickly. Build it by creating views that create schemas on top of the warehouse that separate the full schema out into departments.

Now how much you do further transformations depends on your BI tool. Most BI tools have the ability to create calculated fields and create self-serve data sets. Some tools such as Looker require you to model the data using their own proprietary language to prepare it for analysis. Others allow you to browse multiple schemas at once and combine data however you want, even for an individual chart, potentially using multiple sources of data on a single dashboard.

Whatever your BI tool of choice, consider how to enrich data with calculated fields and join in additional categorical variables that may aid in their department-specific analysis.

Chapter Sixteen

Data Mart Implementation

Data warehouses have numerous schemas that can become difficult to navigate. One department alone such as marketing may have tens if not over a hundred tables; combined with all the tables for sales, finance, HR, production, and customer support, it can get overwhelming. Moving from a data warehouse to data marts makes it easier for users to find the data they need for their business process or use case.

Data marts can be created in three steps.

Views on the Data Warehouse

Create new views by selecting the relevant data from the data warehouse (Figure 16.1) to build out each data mart:

Figure 16.1

```
CREATE VIEW mart_view
SELECT
  *
FROM
  DataWarehouse.View
```

Most if not all of the cleaning should have occurred when going from the lake to the warehouse; if there is a cleanliness issue, address it with modeling in the warehouse stage.

Additional modeling to create aggregations for performance reasons is fine, but remember it does limit analysis. Also, combining data to make it even easier to analyze is common in marts. For combining data we still recommend using the wide table approach.

Segment Tables

Determine how to split the data into different data marts.

Common organizational ways include:

- Department
- Product line
- Use case
- Access level
- Security considerations

Examples of splitting by business process:

- Lead to cash
- Product analytics
- Hire to retire

Create a matrix that contains the table names and the segments you are splitting up the data by to determine which group has access to what. Then create the relevant views for each data mart.

Access Update

Prior to implementing data marts, all of the different segments of a business had access only to the data warehouse through a BI tool. Continuing to provide everyone access to the warehouse schema and the mart schemas helps people find answers quickly and gives them the tools to dig in deeper to the data if they so choose.

Chapter Seventeen

Data Mart Maintenance

Now that the data marts are set up, they will need ongoing maintenance to get the most out of your data. The first step is to establish a mart lead per mart who will be responsible for carrying out the maintenance tasks for each mart:

- Educate team.
- Identify issues.
- Identify new needs.

Mart leads are ideally part of the business unit that needs the mart. They know the context for the data; if Facebook ads spike in their conversion rate, they should be the ones who'd know "that's because we just cut our spend in half and removed the nonperforming ads." They can communicate with the warehouse lead about their teams' data needs and then communicate and educate the team about using their mart.

They are responsible for identifying issues in the data that exist in their mart. They also should be the ones creating requests to get more data sources or tables added to their mart. They also should be part of the workflow/ticket system and be able to teach others and maybe even respond themselves to tickets/data requests.

Educate Team

Different teams have different needs, but some common threads include teaching SQL skills or how to use your BI tool. We wrote a book on how to teach SQL to help with explaining how JOINs, aggregations, and subqueries work. These concepts are not intuitive to most business users; however, they can be taught in a relatively short time frame.

Mart leads should document and share data quirks that show up in common queries. Note, however, that the warehouse lead should try to address these quirks with modeling at the data warehouse stage.

Identifies Issues

The mart lead should investigate anything counterintuitive about the data and then, based on their findings, relay back to the warehouse lead to get the issue addressed.

Spikes

When metrics spike above or below their average, investigate the data and potential causal factors. When looking at the data, try segmenting it in different ways to see if there is a common factor in what drove it up. Determining potential causal factors can be more difficult. Check for bugs in your tracking, check with marketing to see if any new campaigns were launched, and check third-party tools/systems (Google search algorithm, an API is down, etc.) that could affect this metric (Figure 17.1).

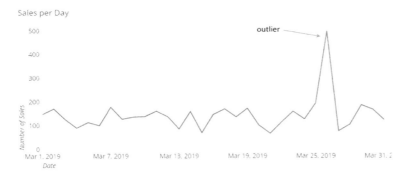

Figure 17.1 An outlier identified in a sales-per-day line graph.

No Spikes

Another point of interest is numbers that are not changing even though changes have been made. When launching a new marketing campaign and the numbers are not going up, that could be due to a bug or poor campaign performance. They should be investigated in that order. Often the tracking was not set up correctly or the link in the advertisement was going to the wrong place (Figure 17.2).

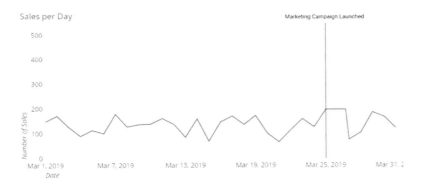

Figure 17.2 A date marked representing when a marketing campaign launched.

No New Data

When queries stop producing data after a specific date, investigate it. It may be a bug, a renamed field, or a data source changed. These problems are more common than expected. For instance, when updating a URL of the data associated with a previous one, it might be cut off (Figure 17.3). However, it is possible to work around these types of problems with SQL.

For example, when Chartio moved its URL from Chart.io to Chartio .com we needed to use:

```
SELECT
  CASE
        WHEN page_tracking.url LIKE 'www.chart.io'
              THEN 'www.chartio.com'
        ELSE page_tracking.url
        END AS "page",
   to_char(page_tracking.viewed_at_date, 'YYYY-MM') AS
   "month",
   COUNT(distinct page_tracking.view_id) AS "views"
FROM
  ga.page_tracking
GROUP BY
  1
ORDER BY
  2 ASC
```

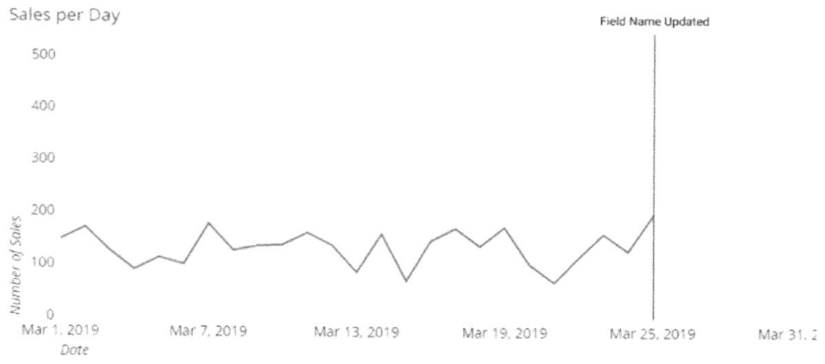

Figure 17.3 A point in time marked when a field name was updated.

It's possible to implement this type of solution as a more permanent fix at the data warehouse stage by updating the relevant view. One note of warning here is that sometimes it's necessary to preserve the historical continuity of the name change by using a date threshold, so think through the implications before making this modeling decision. Consult the warehouse lead or the engineers to find out what is going on and get help fixing it correctly.

Another common issue is that the number of rows a query is returning might be getting limited by the BI tool you are using. Double-check if there is a limit and if you are at it. Most BI tools will let you manually adjust this limit higher so you can get the rest of the data.

All Queries on a Data Source Are Erroring Out

Errors like this happen for a few reasons:

- Deprecation of the source.
- The source had an update changing its data structure.
- A bug somewhere in the process providing the data.

Errors with data sources are something to quickly communicate to the team to prevent a ton of wasted queries and frustrated users.

Slow Queries

Relay slow-running queries to the warehouse lead so that they can investigate creating new views at the data warehouse level. Others can then use this newly formed view. If mart leads are technically savvy, they can begin to explore the company's dbt project and make a PR. A simple one to do would be to switch a view they are using in the mart to a materialized view. While this may not improve the speed right away, it will be a great conversation starter between the mart and warehouse lead about what can be done to improve performance (Figure 17.4).

MART

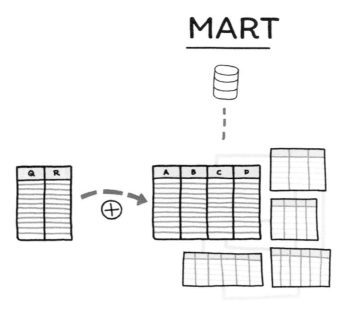

Figure 17.4 The process of adding new columns to a data mart.

Identify New Needs

Data is never a static thing. As new features roll out, so do new tools and objectives, with new data requirements emerging. Do not assume that your mart updates when any of these changes happen. It's necessary to proactively request for these updates to be reflected in the data mart from the warehouse lead. We can leverage the ticketing system we set up in the data warehouse stage to surface these concerns.

Help Track Success

A big role of the mart lead can be to help those on the team think through (analytically) what they're trying to accomplish and how they'd like to track it. Basically, help them set up the dashboards they need. Often people need help there and need a good review once it's done to see that it's correct and useful. They'll also have more experience and knowledge to know what's not being tracked or is not available that maybe should be and make that request.

Chapter Eighteen

Modern versus Traditional Data Stacks: What's Changed?

What's Changed?

This book intentionally outlines how to create a modern stack in a straightforward way, but for those who've been in data for years, some of it may be controversial. Many of these strategies will be known to you, but few have been fully published. We want to broaden the conversation on data modeling and orient the collective goal of analytics toward helping others leverage data for insights.

Many things have changed in the data space that has allowed us to become less technologically constrained and more user-focused. The main driving forces of change in data are increasing volume, demand, and user base, coupled with the great decrease in cost.

Storage and Compute Continues to Drop in Price Rapidly

Costs have been plummeting for storing and computing data. The main things driving down these costs are breakthroughs in both architecture and hardware over the past few decades.

Architecture

- Cloud—things are cheap and easily accessed and scaled

- C-Store—column-oriented databases

- Massively Parallel Processing (MPP)

- Separation of storage and compute

Hardware

- SSD

- Vectorized processing (GPUs and now CPUs)

- Continued lowering of storage and compute hardware costs

These advances have made optimizing for storage and performance not as valuable anymore.

Data Lakes Were Added to the Stack and ELT Replaced ETL

Data lakes are a stable stopping point and much less prone to errors. Also if you have to redo things in the model, you don't have to go back and extract and load again from those sources to get the original raw data. You've already got it. It can save big costs and time and enable flexibility.

Also, this allows you to do the modeling in simple SQL, and makes it so job analysts (who are the end users of this data) can do quite well, rather than rely on data engineers.

Data Is Increasingly Democratized

Everyone wants data in order to support their decision making. This means shifting the end user of data from analysts to everybody. This demand has caused an explosion of problem-specific data tools, and for every SaaS tool you have to spin off data that could be used. These additional data sources are now part of the stack, and the ELT process to get them to the lake is critical to making organizations data driven.

Chapter Nineteen

Row- versus Column-Oriented Database

We wanted to spend a bit of time talking about why columnar databases are more performant for analytics, since this will be at the center of your data stack. There are two ways to organize relational databases:

- Row-oriented
- Column-oriented (also known as columnar or C-store)

Row-oriented databases are databases that organize data by record, keeping all of the data associated with a record next to each other in memory. Row-oriented databases are the traditional way of organizing data and still provide some key benefits for storing data quickly. They are optimized for reading and writing rows efficiently.

Common row-oriented databases:

- Postgres
- MySQL

Column-oriented databases are databases that organize data by field, keeping all of the data associated with a field next to each other in memory. Columnar databases have grown in popularity and provide performance advantages to querying data. They are optimized for reading and computing on columns efficiently.

Common column-oriented databases:

- Redshift
- BigQuery
- Snowflake

Row-Oriented Databases

Traditional database management systems were created to store data. They are optimized to read and write a single row of data, which leads to a series of design choices, including having a row store architecture.

In a row store, or row-oriented database, the data is stored row by row, such that the first column of a row will be next to the last column of the previous row.

For instance, let's take the Facebook_Friends data in Table 19.1.

TABLE 19.1   Facebook_Friends

Name	City	Age
Matt	Los Angeles	27
Dave	San Francisco	30
Tim	Oakland	33

This data would be stored on a disk in a row-oriented database and ordered row by row as in Table 19.2.

TABLE 19.2

Matt	Los Angeles	27	Dave	San Francisco	30	Tim	Oakland	33

This allows the database to write a row quickly because all that needs to be done is to tack on another row to the end of the data.

Writing to Row Store Databases

Let's use the data stored in a database (Table 19.3).

TABLE 19.3

Matt	Los Angeles	27	Dave	San Francisco	30	Tim	Oakland	33

If we want to add a new record (Table 19.4), we can just append it to the end of the current data (Table 19.5).

TABLE 19.4

Jen	Vancouver	30

TABLE 19.5

Matt	Los Angeles	27	Dave	San Francisco	30	Tim	Oakland	33	Jen	Vancouver	30

Row-oriented databases are still commonly used for Online Transactional Processing (OLTP) style applications since they can manage writes to the database well. However, another use case for databases is to analyze the data within them. Online Analytical Processing (OLAP) requires a database that can support ad-hoc querying. For analysis, row-oriented databases are slower than C-store databases.

Reading from Row Store Databases

Row-oriented databases are fast at retrieving a row or a set of rows but, when performing an aggregation, they bring extra data (columns) into memory. This is slower than only selecting the columns that are needed for the aggregation. In addition the number of disks the row-oriented database might need to access is typically more.

Extra Data into Memory

Say we want to get the sum of ages from the Facebook_Friends data. To do this we need to load all nine of these pieces of data into memory and then pull out the relevant data for the aggregation (Table 19.6).

TABLE 19.6

Matt	Los Angeles	27	Dave	San Francisco	30	Tim	Oakland	33

This is wasted computing time.

Column-Oriented Databases

Data warehouses were created in order to support analyzing data. These types of databases are read optimized.

In a C-Store, columnar, or column-oriented database, the data is stored such that each row of a column will be next to other rows from that same column.

Let's look at the same data set again (Table 19.7) and see how it is stored in a column-oriented database. A table is stored one column at a time and ordered row by row (Table 19.8).

TABLE 19.7   Facebook_Friends

Name	City	Age
Matt	Los Angeles	27
Dave	San Francisco	30
Tim	Oakland	33

TABLE 19.8

Matt	Dave	Tim	Los Angeles	San Francisco	Oakland	27	30	33

Writing to a Column Store Databases

If we want to add a new record (Table 19.9), we have to navigate around the data to plug each column into where it should be (Table 19.10), which is not as efficient as a row-oriented database.

TABLE 19.9

Jen	Vancouver	30

TABLE 19.10

Matt	Dave	Tim	Jen	Los Angeles	San Francisco	Oakland	Vancouver	27	30	33	30

Reading from a Column Store Database

To get the sum of the ages, the computer only needs to go to one disk (Disk 3) and sum all the values inside of it. No extra memory needs to be pulled in, and it accesses a minimal number of disks.

While this is a slight oversimplification, it illustrates that by organizing data by column the number of disks that will need to be visited will be reduced and the amount of extra data that has to be held in memory is minimized. This greatly increases the overall speed of the computation.

There are other ways in which a column-oriented database can get more performance.

Coding the Data into More Compact Forms

Let's first examine an encoding technique that can be used by row- or column-oriented databases. Take, for example, a column of data with the individual states of the United States. We can use dictionary and bitmap encodings:

- There are 50 states, so we could encode the whole database with 6 bits since this would provide us 64 unique patterns.
- To store the actual abbreviations would require 16 bits since this would provide us with 256 unique patterns for each of the two ASCII characters.
- Worst of all, if we stored the full name, the lengths would be variable, and the amount of bits needed would be a lot more.

Now let's take a look at Run-length encoding. This allows replacement of any sequence of the same value with a count and value indicator. For instance, we can replace aaaab with 4a1b. This becomes even more powerful when creating projections with columns that are sorted since all values that are the same are next to each other.

Compressing the Data

If each piece of data is the same number of bits long, then all of the data can be further compressed to be the number of pieces of data times that number of bits for a single piece of data.

Ordering the Data

When doing ad-hoc queries, there are a number of different sort orders of the data that would improve performance. For instance, we might want data listed by date, both ascending and descending. We might be looking for a lot of data on a single customer, so ordering by customer could improve performance.

In row-oriented databases, indexes can be created but data is rarely stored in multiple sort orders. However, in column-oriented databases the data can be stored in an arbitrary number of ways. In fact, there are benefits beyond query performance. These different sort-ordered columns are referred to as projections, and they allow the system to be more fault tolerant, since the data is stored multiple times (Table 19.11).

TABLE 19.11

Original Database (WS)			Name Ordered ASC (RS)			Name Ordered DESC (RS)		
Disk 1			Disk 1			Disk 1		
Name			Name			Name		
Matt	Dave	Tim	Dave	Matt	Tim	Tim	Matt	Dave
Disk 2			Disk 2			Disk 2		
City			City			City		
Los Angeles	San Francisco	Oakland	San Francisco	Los Angeles	Oakland	Oakland	Los Angeles	San Francisco
Disk 3			Disk 3			Disk 3		
Age			Age			Age		
27	30	33	30	27	33	33	27	30

This seems like a complicated set of tables to update, and it is. This is why the architecture of a C-store database has a writeable store (WS) and a read-optimized store (RS). The writeable store has the data sorted in the order it was added to make adding data into it easier. We can easily append the relevant fields to our database as seen in Table 19.12.

TABLE 19.12

Original Database (WS)			
Disk 1			
Name			
Matt	Dave	Tim	Jen
Disk 2			
City			
Los Angeles	San Francisco	Oakland	Vancouver
Disk 3			
Age			
27	30	33	30

Then the read-optimized store can have multiple projections. It then has a tuple mover that manages the relevant updates from the WS to the RS. It has to navigate the multiple projections and insert the data in the proper places (Table 19.13).

This architecture means that while the data is being updated from the WS to the RS, the partially added data must be ignored by queries to the RS until the update is complete.

TABLE 19.13

Name Ordered ASC (RS)			
Disk 1			
Name			
Dave	Jen	Matt	Tim
Disk 2			
City			
San Francisco	Vancouver	Los Angeles	Oakland
Disk 3			
Age			
30	30	27	33

Name Ordered DESC (RS)			
Disk 1			
Name			
Tim	Matt	Jen	Dave
Disk 2			
City			
Oakland	Los Angeles	Vancouver	San Francisco
Disk 3			
Age			
33	27	30	30

Summary

Column-oriented databases came out with a 2005 paper explaining the design that Redshift, BigQuery, and Snowflake are all built upon. It's why they all have about the same performance and relative costs. This column-oriented database is being used by most major providers of cloud data warehouses. This has become the dominant architecture in relational databases to support OLAP.

Chapter Twenty

Style Guide Example

Going through and creating a clean data warehouse and marts makes the data easier to understand for everyone. As an organization grows, more than one person will help clean and transform the data. There are aspects of cleaning that are subjective, and we need to codify what we want to happen. For example, we will want to rename a column to make it more readable, but should we use snake case (e.g. example_new_column) or camel case (e.g. ExampleNewColumn)? In the book we said snake case, but this is a judgment call and you could go with another convention.

Document cleaning goals and stylistic preferences in a style guide so that we clean the data consistently and others can help.

We have provided sample style guides at the end of the chapter.

Simplify

It's quite common for raw data to be extremely complicated. When data comes into existence, in most cases, it's intended to be used by applications and not directly by business users. Taking time to simplify data significantly improves the ability for business users to successfully query it.

Only Include Fields That Have an Apparent Analytical Purpose

If your system makes it easy to update/add new columns, it's best to start modeling with only the most relevant columns, excluding any columns that have no direct or apparent analytical purpose.

Extract Relevant Data from Complex Data Tpes

Application data sources may contain JSON, arrays, Hstore, and other complex data types. These are typically hard to query from business intelligence tools in their raw form. However, relevant data can be extracted into new columns, which can be queried easily.

Suppose a table named books contains an id column and the following JSON column:

```
{
 title: "Moby Dick",
 author: "Herman Melville",
 genres: \["novel", "fiction"\]
}
```

The resulting modeled books table would contain an id, title, and author columns. Genres could be modeled as an independent table, reduced to a single genre based on custom rules or some other method.

Change Flags and Cryptic Abbreviations to Meaningful Values

It's common for application databases to have flags or cryptic abbreviations in columns that work well for an application to reference.

These can be impossible for a business user to interpret. It's essential to transform these values into natural, human-readable values, for example:

Transform Boolean values 0 and 1 to relevant strings, such as true and false or on and off.

Change Boolean field names to be descriptive and start with is_ or has_. It is challenging to interpret Boolean field names when they are ambiguous, such as "inactive," "subscribed," or "paid."

Transform flag values into relevant strings by joining to a dimension table or remapping the data. Avoid creating the same "case when" statement in multiple places. If a column billing_status has three discrete values (i.e. 0, 1, 2) that represent some status, transform them into a relevant business concept such as "Active," "Not Active," or "Delinquent."

Transform hard-to-interpret values into easy-to-understand values.

Denormalize Where Beneficial

Applications typically have highly normalized tables to prevent duplicates, reduce space, and make modifications easier. Excessive normalization typically makes it harder for business users to browse the schema, usually due to the complexity of the joins. Building wider tables wherever appropriate and collapsing common concepts into a single table help to reduce excessive joins. Some examples include:

- Combine the sources, sources_redshift, sources_postgres, and sources_mysql tables into a single source table with the lowest common denominator of values that make sense for a business user.
- Combine the users and addresses tables into a single users table since addresses are meaningless on their own.

Denormalization requires trial and error and takes time to get it right.

Clean

Data is messy and frequently requires cleaning to ensure accurate results. Cleaning prevents common problems that might cause a query to produce incorrect results.

Attempt to Eliminate NULLs

NULL values have unexpected consequences in SQL (is "string" <> NULL?). It's best to replace all NULLs with values. Some examples:

- Change all NULL values in the first_name column to the string Blank.
- Change all NULL values in the last_login_type column to the string Never Logged In for customers that have never logged in.

Fix Common Data Inconsistencies

Bad data always makes its way into raw data sources. Whether it is misspellings or just junk data, it is essential to clean up the data as much as possible. Some examples:

Transform state names that have a mix of abbreviations, full names, and junk data into a single, consistent format such as the full state name.

Phone numbers might be garbage text entered by users to avoid getting phone calls.

Remove Irrelevant Data

Rows that are irrelevant for various reasons should be removed entirely from the data set. Examples include:

- Employee testing
- Fraud or spam
- Inactive

The exception is when analyzing fraud or spam data (given the above examples), but in most cases, rows that are never present from a query can be removed during modeling.

Standardize Data Types

Modeling is a great time to change data types to more appropriate types. Unix timestamps could be converted from int columns to datetime, for example.

Naming Conventions

There are a variety of naming conventions used for tables, columns, and values. Creating a standard for schema resources improves the usability for others to find and understand the data they need.

Plural Table Names

Pluralization of table names creates an easy-to-identify distinction from columns and other schema resources when communicating. For example, change the title of a table of leads named "Lead" to "Leads." When there are more than two words, only pluralize the last word: opportunity_histories.

Singular Column Names

A column name such as "emails" should be titled "email," not "emails." Singular names make it easy to distinguish between tables and columns.

id as Primary Key

A simple numeric primary key labeled "id" is the standard for all tables. The "id" convention uniquely identifies the primary key and each row:

```
foreign keys follow [tablename]_[id] format
```

Foreign keys should follow this format to make the relationships to other tables very clear. If there are two foreign keys related to the same table, prepend a name to them following the format:

```
\[uniquename\]_\[tablename\]_\[id\].
```

An accounts table linking to a users table with both a billing contact and a main owner would look like this:

```
Accounts
owner_user_id
Billing_contact_user_id
```

Lowercase, Underscored Naming

The data model needs to be easily editable with SQL, so avoiding the shift key allows faster development of queries. Therefore, we should attempt to have column names like id, first_name, last_name, and last_login_type instead of more human-readable forms in the model. In addition, spaced names such as first name, last name, and last login type will break the SQL code. Use underscores for any spaces between words.

Share It

Publish a style guide and distribute it among employees to make adoption of known terms much easier. Collect feedback and grow it as new scenarios emerge. Check out some other public examples of style guides for inspiration:

- https://about.gitlab.com/handbook/business-ops/data-team/platform/sql-style-guide/#other-sql-style-guides
- https://github.com/brooklyn-data/co/blob/master/sql_style_guide.md
- https://github.com/fishtown-analytics/corp/blob/master/dbt_coding_conventions.md#sql-style-guide

Chapter Twenty-One

Building an SST Example

To build a data warehouse you need to determine what tables and fields you will be including in it. Everyone's data sources are different, so there is no one right way. We will share some iterations we went through several years ago to get from the lake to the warehouse stage and how we responded to feedback and challenges.

First Attempt—Same Tables with Prefixes

In the original design of our data warehouse, we envisioned the schema to include all the needed tables from our raw sources: Chartio database, Salesforce, Stripe, Zendesk, Jira, Intercom, and Hubspot.

At this point there was no concept of a "staging schema" or "base models," so we would query the raw tables and do data cleanup and transformation on them to build the SST. Because the different sources could have tables with the same names, each table would be prefixed with the name of the original source. Prefixing the table names with their underlying source also helps the user know where the data is coming from and keeps the schema organized as well.

Here is a sample of the tables in this schema:

- Chartio Charts
- Chartio Dashboards
- Chartio Organizations
- Chartio Users
- Intercom Admins
- Intercom Conversations
- Intercom Users
- Jira Issues
- Salesforce Contacts
- Salesforce Leads

What Tables Did We Keep?

In order to choose what tables to bring into the SST, we created a spreadsheet of the list of tables from each source and went through them one by one making the call on whether or not to add it to the SST (Figure 21.1).

Considering we were already familiar with most of the data ourselves, for some tables it was obvious that it was needed based on our prior usage and understanding of the data. For sources we were not as familiar with, we consulted the owners of the tools for information on what tables are needed. For example, our revenue ops manager was a huge resource in telling us what tables were needed from Hubspot and what tables the marketing team uses from Salesforce.

For a select number of tables we were unsure of, we ran internal usage reports to see if there were any existing charts querying those tables (Figure 21.2).

If there were no charts or only archived dashboards querying those tables, it was safe to assume that they wouldn't be needed.

	Tables	Needed?	Status	Comments		17	27
2	Active Organization Users	Y	don't need ar	don't need anymore, we have the org to users table			
3	Admin Api Serviceaccount	Y	In PR				
4	Alerts Alert	Y	In model				
5	Alerts Alert Recipient Teams	Y	In model				
6	Alerts Alert Recipient Users	Y	In model	Teams and Users table combined			
7	Auth User	?		Idk what this is used for			
8	Basic Org Info	N					
9	Chart	Y	In PR	*adding columns to the original from Aaron*			
10	Chart Pipeline Steps	N		custom table in Chartio is erroring out			
11	Chart settings	N		info should be put in Chart table			
12	Comments Comment	Y	In model				
13	Comments Thread	N		not useful			
14	Comments Threaduser	N		not useful			
15	Customer Success Agent	N		CSE field in Starfish			
16	Dashboard	Y	In PR	*making slight modifications to aliases, adding new columns*			
17	Dashboard Datasources	?		custom table in Chartio created by Jeff/Tim			
18	Dashboard Envar	Y	In PR				
19	Dashboard Filter	?		maybe later, the data is really specific (correlates with Dimension and Measure tables. th			
20	Dashboard Theme	Y	In PR	I have used this table once			
21	Dashboard Dashboardthumbnail	N					
22	Dashboards Dashboarduseractions	Y	In model				
23	Dashboards Pastquery	N		I don't understand what data is in here			
24	Dashboards Report	Y	In PR	minor changes to Aaron's			
25	Dashboards Report Recipient Teams	Y	In PR	*Jaime helping me combine these two*			
26	Dashboard Report Recipients Users	Y	In model				
27	Dashboards Snapshot	Y	In PR				
28	Dataset	Y	In PR	*added one column*			
29	Datastore	N		maybe for eng??			
30	Datastore Table	Y	In PR				
31	Datastorerefresh	N		info in Datastore Table table, except for status message			
32	Dimension	Y	In model	the columns in the model are very basic. can add more later if needed			

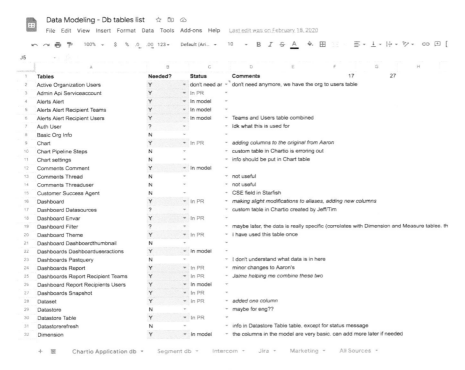

Figure 21.1 Table survey in a spreadsheet.

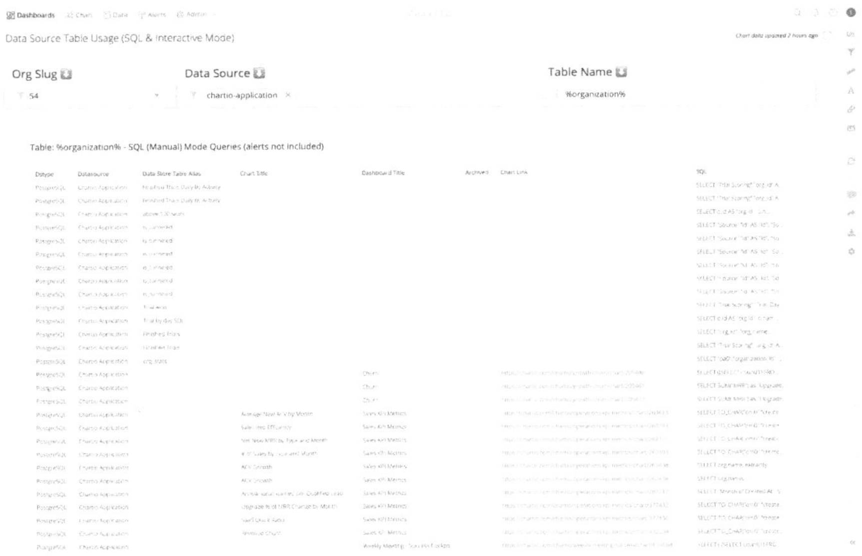

Figure 21.2 Custom query for internal usage within a visual SQL UI.
Source: Data Grip

It's important to note that when we went through the tables and decided which ones to add to the SST, we recognized it was a process and that we were taking our best guess to start. There will be many iterations of an SST, and as users start using it and building charts off of it they will find additional tables that they will need to add.

What Tables Did We Not Include?

For the tables we did not include in the SST, we took into consideration whether the data in the table was up to date, useful, and relevant. Tables that contained very detailed information that was only queried once in a blue moon by an engineer, for example, would not need to be in the SST as it's not widely used and we didn't want to clutter the SST with every possible table. We found tables in our database that were also outdated or contained duplicate data to other tables; these were left out as well.

What Columns Did We Keep?

The process to decide what columns to keep in a given table was similar to deciding what tables to keep. DataGrip made it easy to generate a huge Select statement for a table by selecting all of its columns with the Expand column list feature (Figures 21.3, 21.4, and 21.5).

From there, we would query all of the columns from a table and examine the first 10 to 15 rows to see what was in each column and decide whether or not that data was useful. For some tables we were unsure of, we ran usage reports or checked in Chartio to see whether or not existing charts were using the columns or if it was made visible in the Chartio data source schema to help make the call.

The tool owners also provided valuable insight into what columns were used and what columns were not needed

What Was Not Ideal About It?

Because this schema layout still kept each table associated with their original source, to query data across sources you would need

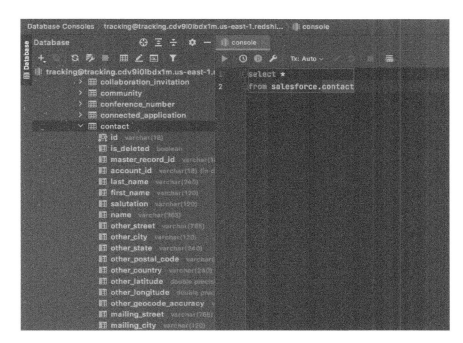

Figure 21.3 Data Grip, an SQL editor.
Source: Data Grip

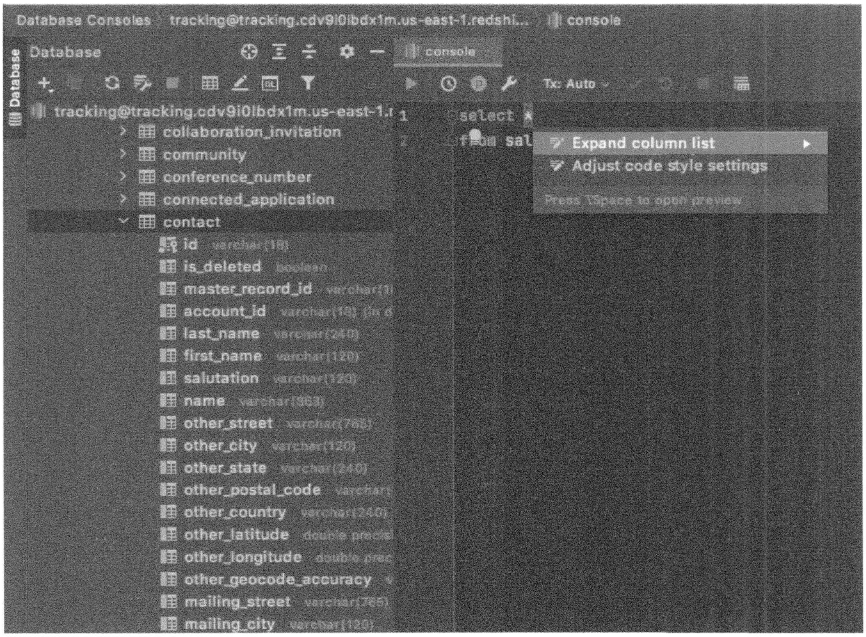

Figure 21.4 An SQL editor with column insert feature selected.
Source: Data Grip

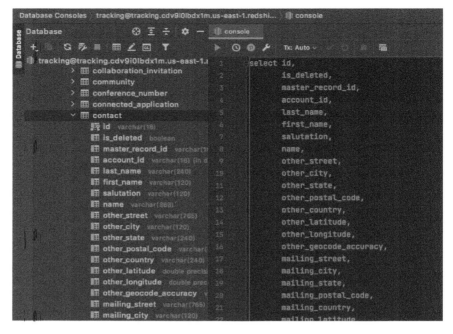

Figure 21.5 An SQL editor with columns inserted.
Source: Data Grip

to go through multiple tables. Looking for all the times a customer wrote into our support channels would require us to query from both the Intercom Conversations and Zendesk Tickets tables, for instance.

We also had similarly named tables such as a Chartio Users, Intercom Users, Salesforce Users, Zendesk Users, and so on.

This schema layout was most useful and easy to use for users who were already familiar with the underlying tools and source data, whereas someone new to Salesforce or Hubspot wouldn't necessarily know where to look for data. After all, it may not be clear what's being tracked as a Salesforce Task versus a Salesforce Event.

What Was the Feedback?

Our customer success team and VP of engineering liked this SST layout. For data-savvy users and users familiar with the original source schemas, it was easy to use because the tables were familiar and the source prefixes made it clear where data from a table was coming from. However, for business users or brand-new users, it was possibly more confusing to locate the data they were looking for. Ultimately, the goal of the SST was to make the data more accessible to the business users, so we still had work to do.

Second Attempt—Operational Schema (Source Agnostic)

In this version of the SST, we would "mask" all the underlying sources the data was coming from and create our own brand-new schema. It's the idea of what if all our tools were built in-house and weren't coming from a variety of places. This means we wouldn't be prefixing the tables with the names of the tools they were coming from, and we would be combining data from multiple sources together into generic tables like "Users," "Tickets," and so forth. Hubspot Contacts and Salesforce Contacts data could also be combined into a single "Contacts" table or even be combined with the "Users" table.

What Tables Did We Keep?

At this point, we had agreed to have a separate staging step prior to the SST. The staging layer looks pretty similar to the first attempt; however, all the underlying source data is contained in their own separate base schemas. The process of deciding what tables to keep is similar to the first attempt. The decision here was more figuring out what tables to combine and what this new schema we were building almost from scratch was going to look like.

There was debate, for instance, on whether to keep the Salesforce Leads and Salesforce Contacts tables separate. Conceptually they both contain data related to people, but operationally they are used in different ways and mean different things to the business. Combining the Leads and Contacts tables with our Chartio Users table would also create one massively wide table with a lot of columns and null values. If we did that, what if we wanted to determine how many of our Salesforce Contacts were also users in our application? Would it be as simple as a Boolean flag "is_chartio_user"? How would we join the tables together? Does it make sense to combine our application "Organizations" table with the Salesforce "Accounts" table?

We had to think through the implications of these decisions given how the columns and fields are treated differently in each source. One instance of this is that in our application, a user can belong to multiple organizations, whereas in Salesforce that user would then exist as separate contacts for each of the associated accounts. We would either have to be fine with having duplicate records in this Users/Contacts table, or just select one of the user records and drop the others (Table 21.1).

TABLE 21.1   Duplicate Records by Email

User Id	Email	SFDC Contact Id
214587	burt.smith@chartio.com	0031M00002mb10U
214587	burt.smith@chartio.com	0031M00003ha82Z
User Id	**Email**	**SFDC Contact Id**
214587	burt.smith@chartio.com	{'0031M00002mb10U', '0031M00003ha82Z'}
User Id	**Email**	**SFDC Contact Id**
214587	burt.smith@chartio.com	0031M00002mb10U

How Did We Make These Decisions?

To determine what this new schema would look like and where it makes sense to combine tables together, there were many whiteboard sessions and sketching out schema diagrams on paper with key stakeholders, which included our CEO, VP of engineering, and VP of customer success. We thought through common use cases from users and how simple or complex a query would need to be in order to answer a question.

What Was Not Ideal About It?

In this approach, we were trying to create our own schema by "combining" the tables and columns of our underlying sources. But obviously since the schemas of each source were different, there were fields from one source that another source wouldn't have, and this created very wide tables with a lot of null values. We had to figure out the complexities of joining tables and combining data together that look totally different in raw form.

To avoid confusion with the raw tables, we also had to consider how to name the tables. Since Salesforce already had the concepts of "Contacts" and "Leads" and "Users," would a combined table be called "People" or something else? A data dictionary would also need to be kept so people can refer to what these new tables mean.

Creating a new schema that was source agnostic also required more time to map out the schema and build the tables.

What Was the Feedback?

Customer success members were more nervous about this approach, because as users already familiar with the raw tables, it would take more education to learn and train others on the new schema. People who were already familiar with the raw tables and the definitions of those tables may find this schema confusing. For business users, this schema would likely be more ideal as it is more business-centric as opposed to source- or product-centric.

Third Attempt—Application Separate, Other Sources Smashed

After much discussion following up on the first attempt and operational schema, we settled on creating a SST that was more Chartio-centric. What that meant was our Chartio application product data would be kept as separate tables to the rest of our source data, which could be considered supplementary tables. Aside from that, this was identical to the operational schema described in the second attempt.

What Tables Did We Keep?

Choosing what tables to add to the SST (similarly to the second attempt) was largely a decision on what tables are the most heavily used. In order to not clog up the SST with an extra long list of tables, in the first iteration we left out tables we thought would only be rarely queried or accessed. If we discovered later that users need some of those tables that weren't included, we could add them.

The process in this attempt was similar to the second attempt in that we had to determine the schema layout and what the tables will look like. Because we agreed on a Chartio-centric approach, the "Organizations" and "Users" tables from our Chartio database were to be separate from our "Accounts" and "Contacts" tables. All the supplementary data from the other sources was to be combined and joined in larger tables where reasonable. We decided on a big "Interactions" table that contained all our ticket and customer touchpoint data, a large "Contacts" table that contained Salesforce Contacts and Leads data, Hubspot Contacts data, and Zendesk and Intercom user data. Since we only use JIRA internally, we kept the JIRA tables separate. And to create an easy mapping of employee ids across systems, we created an "Internal Users" fact table.

What Columns Did We Keep?

In determining what columns to keep particularly when joining tables together, we had to see if columns from one source table could easily map to a column from another source table. For example, Zendesk's "Requester Id" field could be mapped to Intercom's "Author Id" field. Salesforce Contacts and Hubspot Contacts had a few duplicate fields so we didn't need to include both when joining the tables together.

What Was the Feedback?

Direct feedback from our VP of engineering: "I think trying to collapse all the interactions and contacts into a single table is showing signs of weakness in its current form. It's either too generic to be valuable, without enough fields, or too broad, having tons of nulls so you have to be really careful how you query. Totally fine letting this play out to see how things turn out but foresee some issues we will have to work through."

One of our customer success managers expressed that her team often wants to know and track the touchpoints for our customers, but doesn't really care about the channel. They want to know if we've been in contact with them, so it's helpful to have all the information from our various channels together in the Interactions table.

Currently, usage of the SST is still ramping but as more people start using it, cracks have been starting to show. For example, when combining the Salesforce Leads and Contacts data into the generic "Contacts" table, initially we filtered out converted leads to avoid duplicate records. This proved unhelpful to our marketing and sales teams, who care about historical data from converted leads.

Less Planning, More Implementing

In the old days data modelers did a lot of designing. They gathered a lot of requirements to determine their exact use case and created star schemas for business users. We now have the tools and performance to make this a more collaborative endeavor, where a warehouse lead can model and iterate based on feedback. We continue to iterate on our schema to suit our business needs and believe that schema design is an ongoing process.

Especially after creating the staging models for the sources we use in our warehouse, we can try many configurations of tables to see what supports analytics best. Since everything is layered on top of the database, it can be changed on a whim. It takes less pre-thinking (which is largely impossible guessing), less meetings, less restructuring, less architecting, less complexity, and less repetition.

Acknowledgments and Contributions

This book has been a large effort by a number of people and continues to evolve with community involvement. We appreciate everyone's help in making this book a useful guide for people who are building their data stacks.

Thank-yous

I want to give a special thanks to Matt David, the head of the Data School for working on the start of this for so many hours with me. He has project managed, refined ideas, and written the majority of this book and continually recruits community involvement. His passion for educating the masses on data is truly inspirational, and he is a joy to work with.

I also want to thank Tim Miller and Tracy Chow, who contributed to many chapters here and worked many stressful hours on content with me. Thank you, Tim and Tracy, for your constant drive and passion for both learning and educating.

Also I'd like to thank the rest of the Chartio Data Advisor team, who each contributed a chapter and who daily take the learnings in this book directly to our customers.

Thank you, Liz Wikstrom, for your always excellent design and illustrations that honor this book and site. Thank you, Eleanor Preston, for helping me work through this framework on so many customer visits—and persistently waiting for us to get it published!

Thank you, Kostas Paradalis of Blendo, for your input on the chapter on ETL vs ELT. Thank you Tristan for providing feedback on writing the foreword.

And lastly, a big thank-you to our editors, Emilie Schario, Mila Page, and David Yerrington. They got us through the toughest parts of this book and made sure it was clear and accurate.

Index